INDEX TO MAPS

NORTH EASTERN U S A
MAP LOCATION

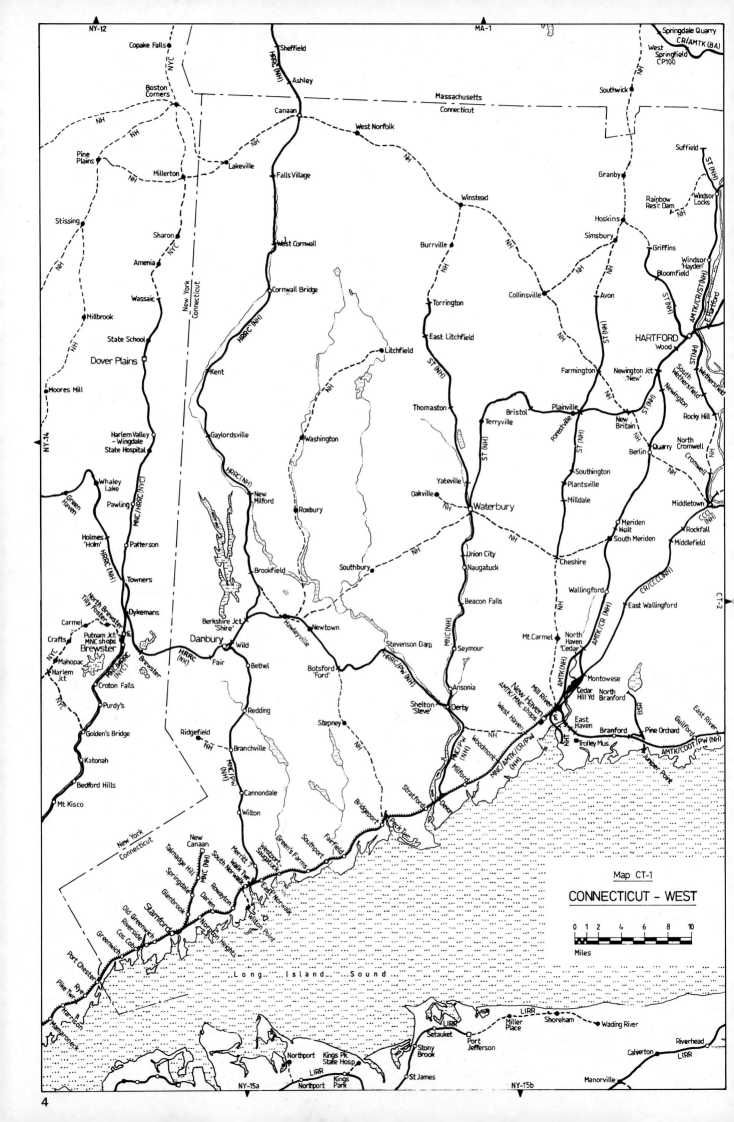

Map CT-1

CONNECTICUT - WEST

0 1 2   4   6   8   10

Miles

4

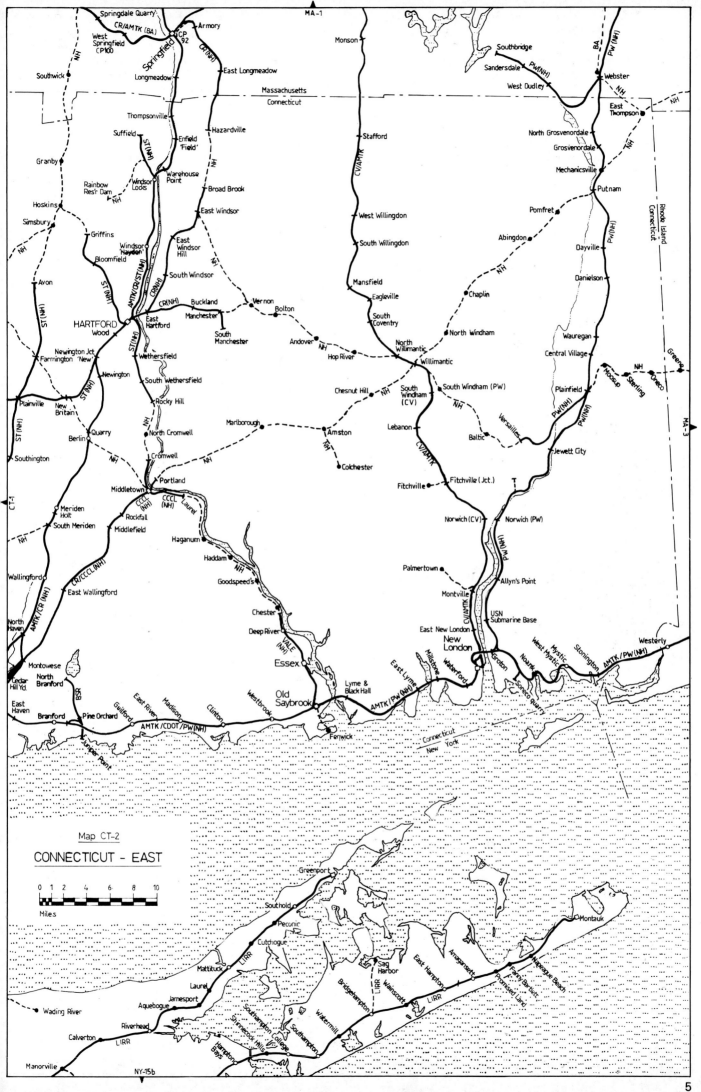

Map CT-2

CONNECTICUT - EAST

0 1 2 4 6 8 10

Miles

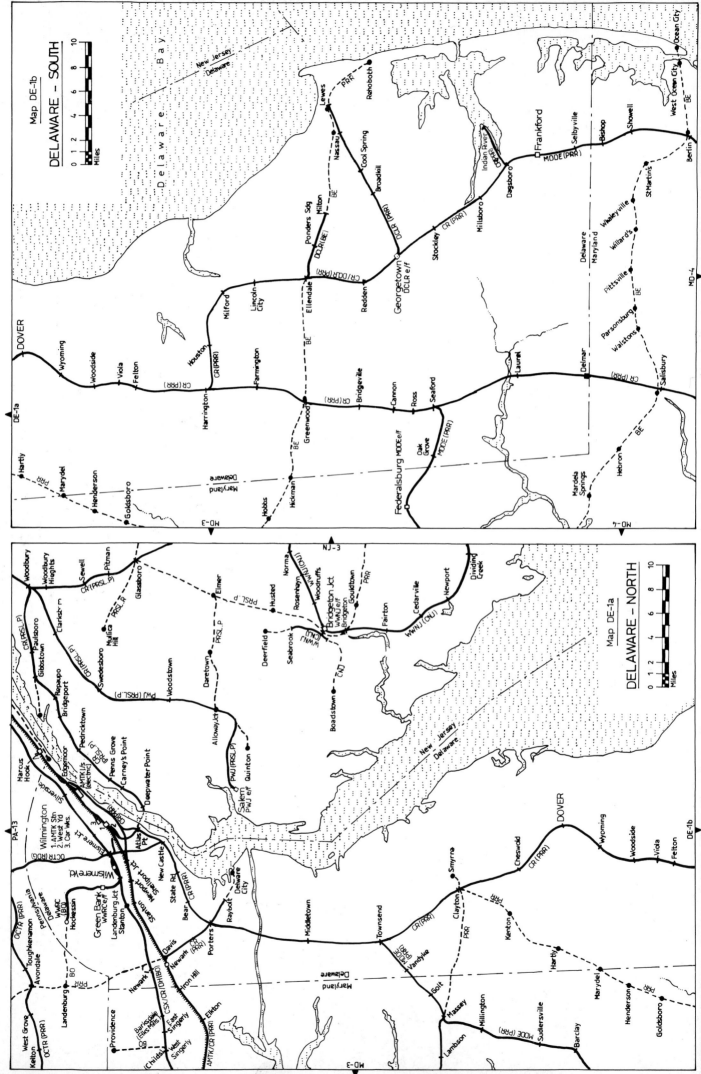

Map DE-1b
DELAWARE - SOUTH

Miles
0 1 2   4   6   8   10

Map DE-1a
DELAWARE - NORTH

Miles
0 1 2   4   6   8   10

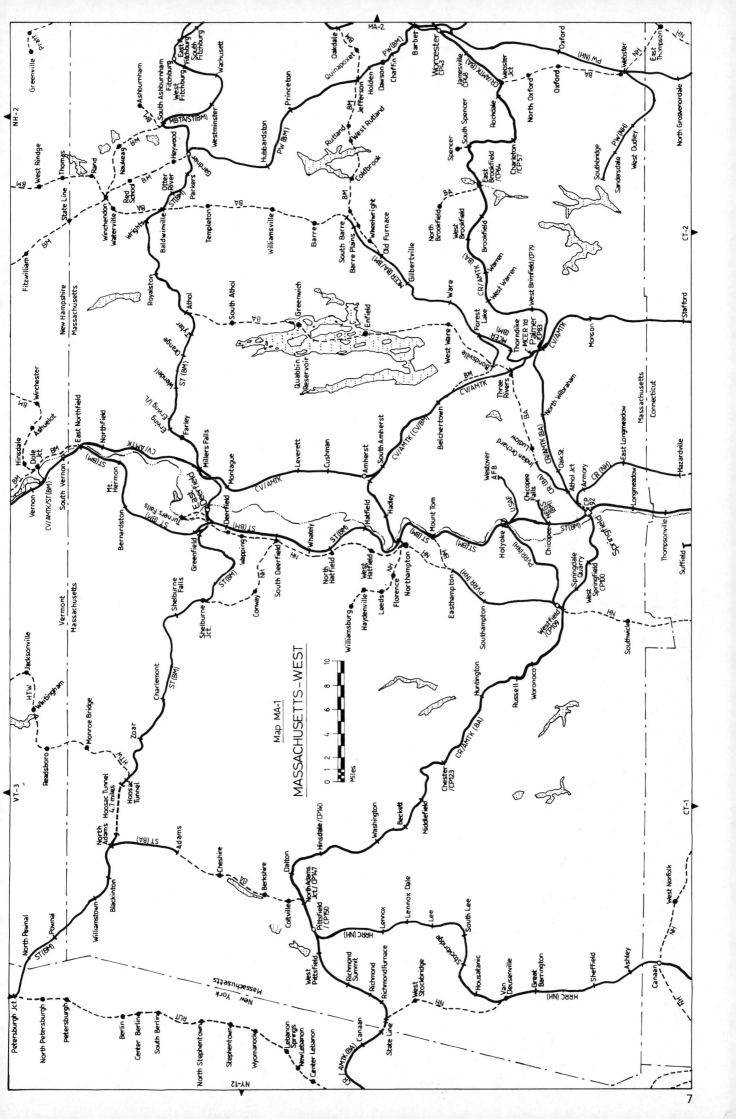

Map MA-1

MASSACHUSETTS – WEST

Miles
0 1 2 4 6 8 10

7

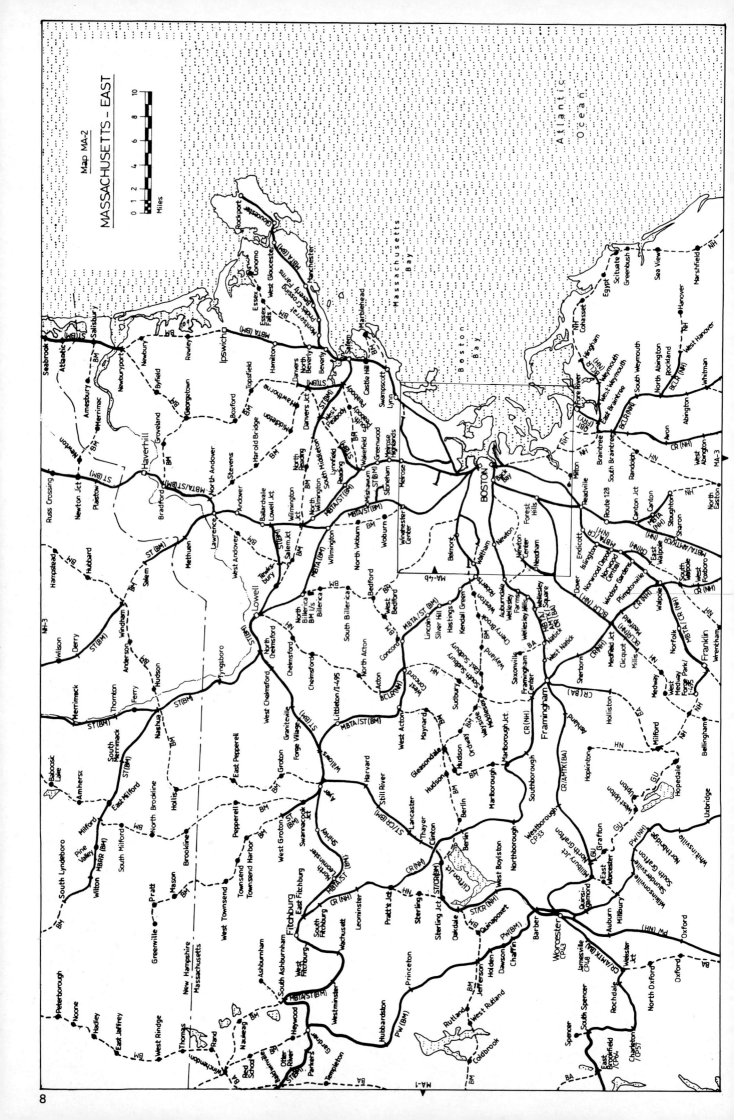

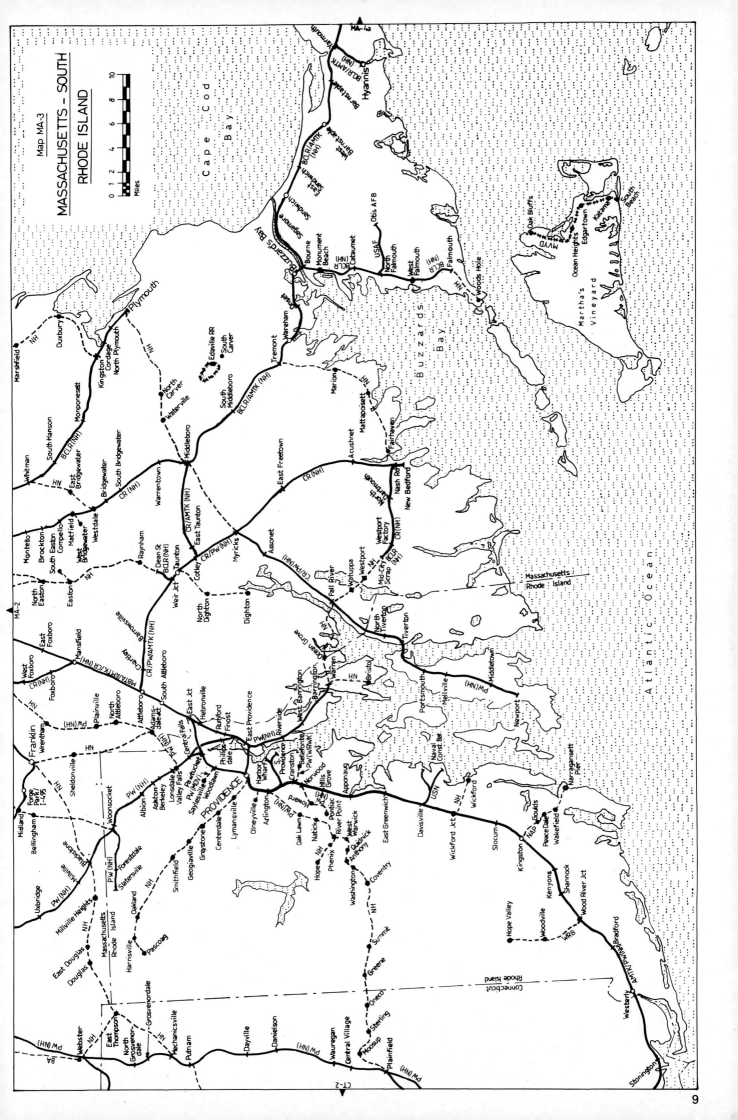

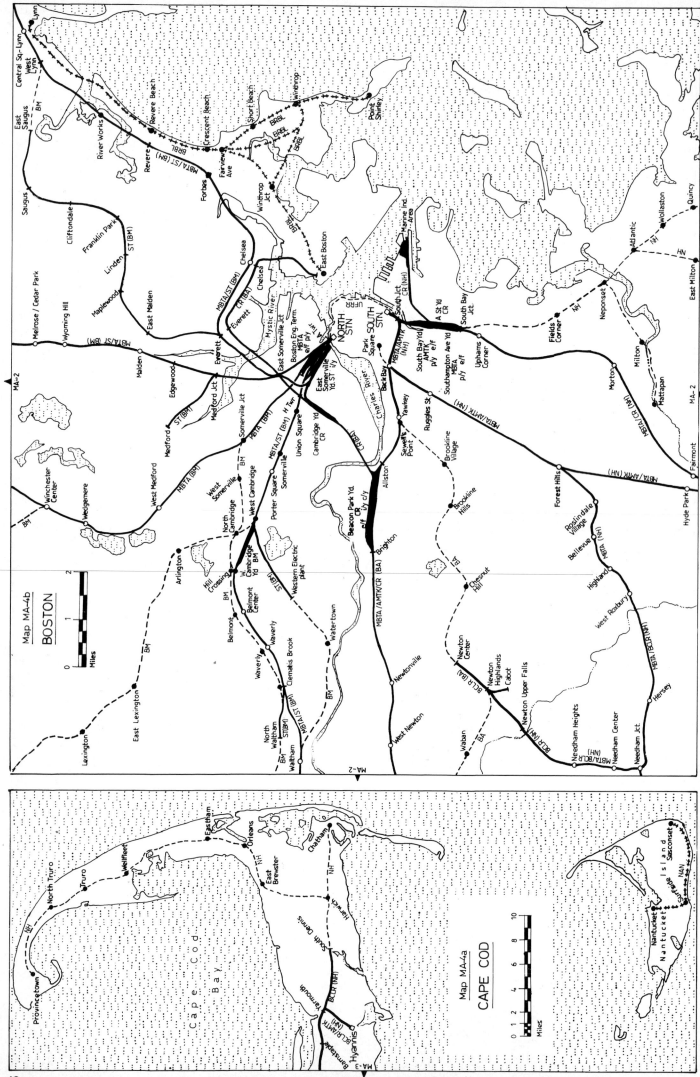

Map MA-4b
BOSTON

Map MA-4a
CAPE COD

10

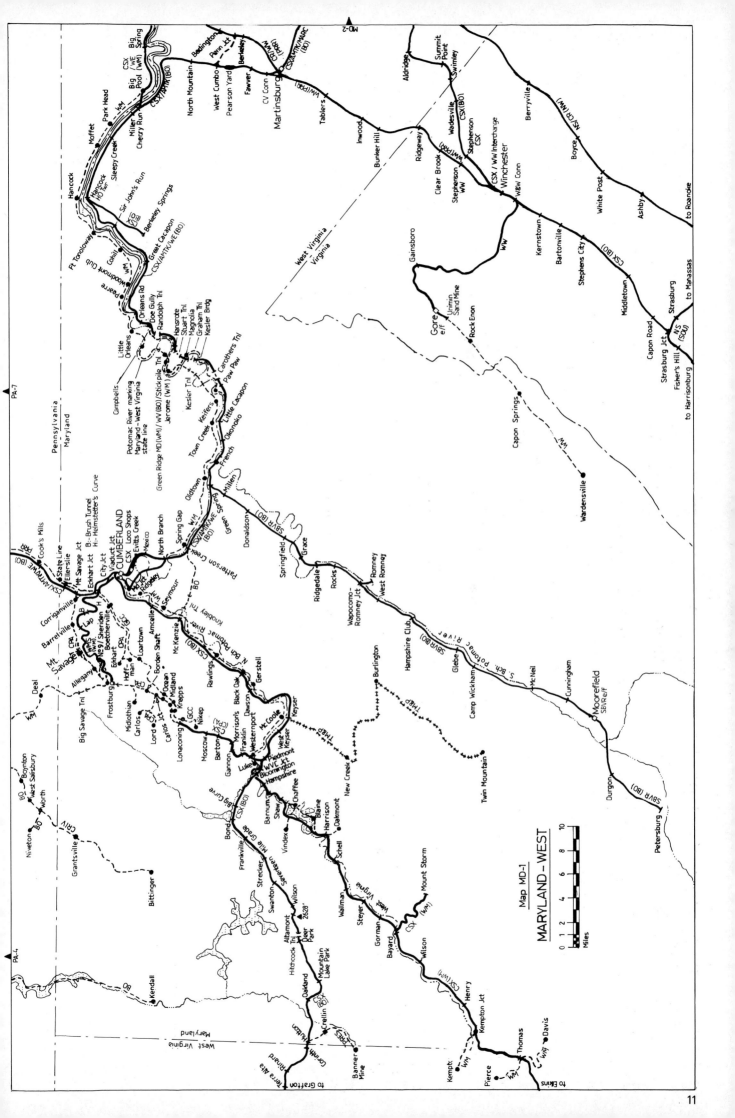

Map MD-1

MARYLAND – WEST

Miles
0 1 2 4 6 8 10

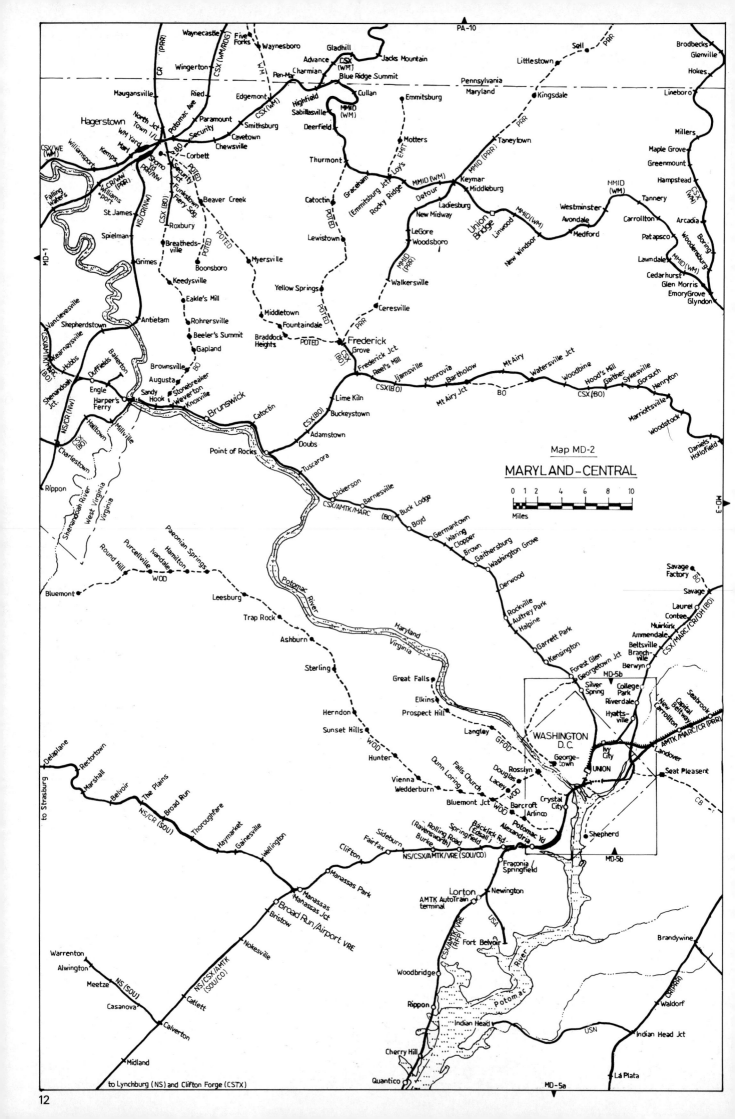

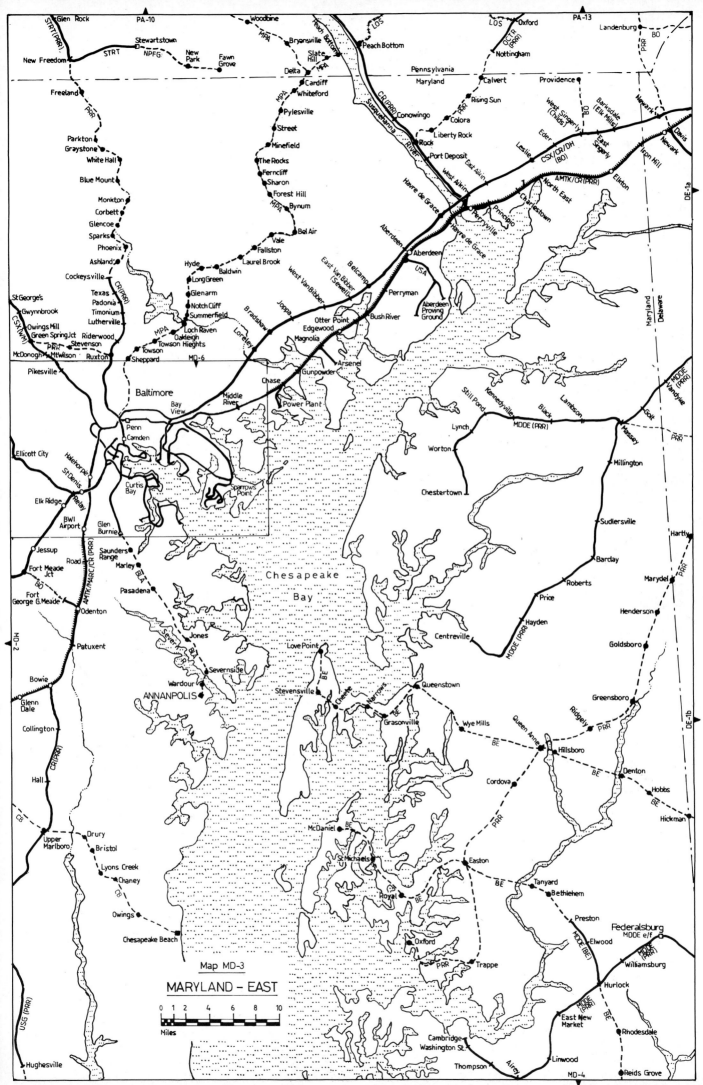

Map MD-3

MARYLAND – EAST

0 1 2 4 6 8 10

Miles

13

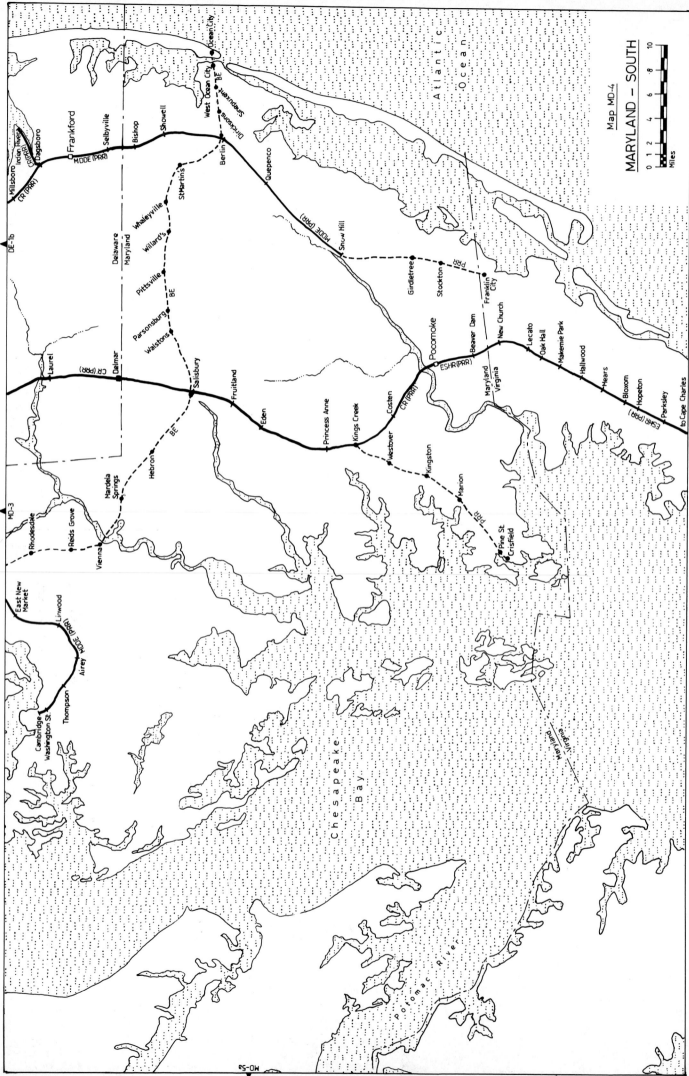

Map MD-4

MARYLAND – SOUTH

14

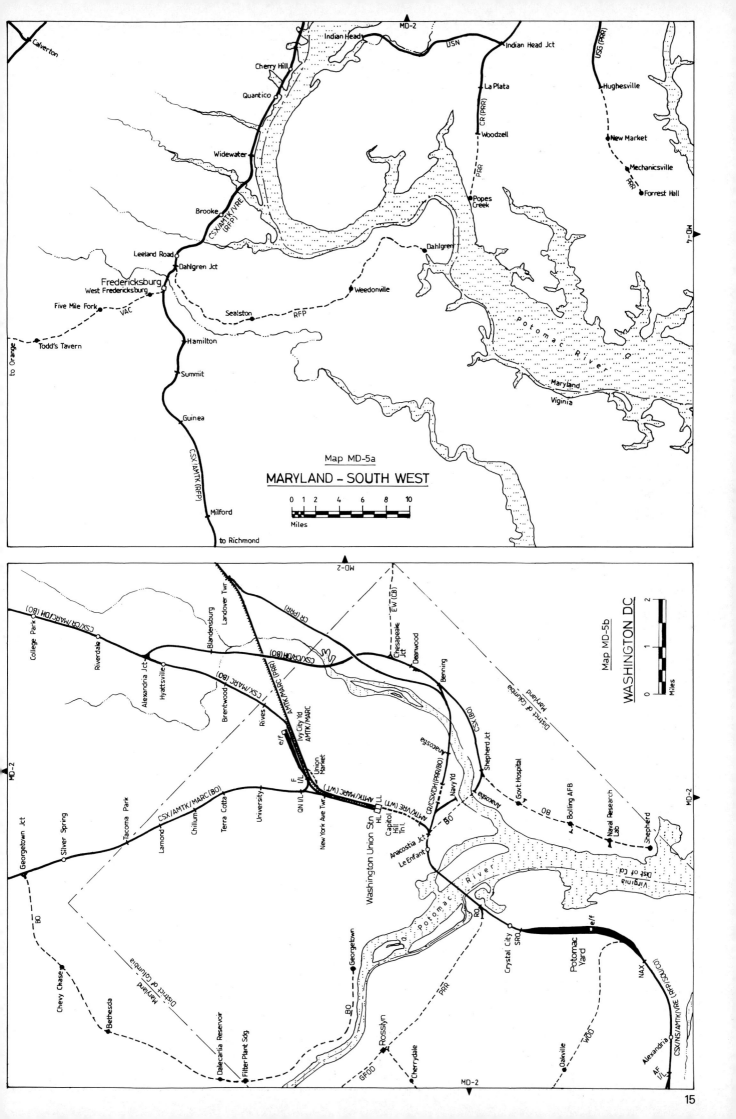

Map MD-5a

MARYLAND – SOUTH WEST

Map labels (Map MD-5a):

Calverton
Indian Head
Cherry Hill
Quantico
Widewater
Brooke
CSX/AMTK/VRE (RFP)
Leeland Road
Dahlgren Jct
Fredericksburg
West Fredericksburg
Five Mile Fork
VAC
Todd's Tavern
to Orange
Hamilton
Summit
Guinea
Sealston
RFP
Weedonville
Dahlgren
CSX/AMTK (RFP)
Milford
to Richmond
USN
Indian Head Jct
La Plata
CR (PRR)
Woodzell
PRR
Popes Creek
USG (PRR)
Hughesville
New Market
Mechanicsville
RGG
Forrest Hall
MD-4
MD-2
Potomac River
Maryland
Viginia

Scale: 0 1 2 4 6 8 10 Miles

Map MD-5b

WASHINGTON DC

Map labels (Map MD-5b):

College Park
CSX/CR/MARC/DH (BO)
Riverdale
Alexandria Jct
Hyattsville
Blandensburg
Landover Twr
CR (PRR)
CSX/CR/DH (BO)
Chesapeake Jct
Deanwood
E W (CB)
Brentwood
CSX/MARC (PRR)
AMTK (MARC)
Rives
e/f
Ivy City Yd AMTK/MARC
Union Market
Benning
CSX (BO)
Shepherd Jct
District of Columbia
Georgetown Jct
MD-2
Silver Spring
Tacoma Park
CSX/AMTK/MARC (BO)
Lamond
Chillum
Terra Cotta
University
QN I/L
F
I/L
New York Ave Twr
AMTK/MARC (WT)
HL
LL
Capitol Hill Tnl.
AMTK/VRE (WT)
Anacostia Jct
Le Enfant
Navy Yd
CR/CSX/DH (PRR/BO)
Anacostia
Shepherd Jct
Govt Hospital
BO
Bolling AFB
Naval Research Lab
Shepherd
Maryland
District of Columbia
BO
Chevy Chase
Bethesda
Dalecarlia Reservoir
Filter Plant Sdg
Georgetown
Potomac River
BO
Rosslyn
GFOD
Cherrydale
MD-2
Anacostia Jct
RO
Crystal City
SRO
e/f
Potomac Yard
NAX
Alexandria
CSX/NS/AMTK (RFP)
Oakville
WDT
AF I/L
CSX/AMTK/VRE (RFP/SOU/CO)
PRR
Virginia
Dist of Col
MD-2

Scale: 0 1 2 Miles

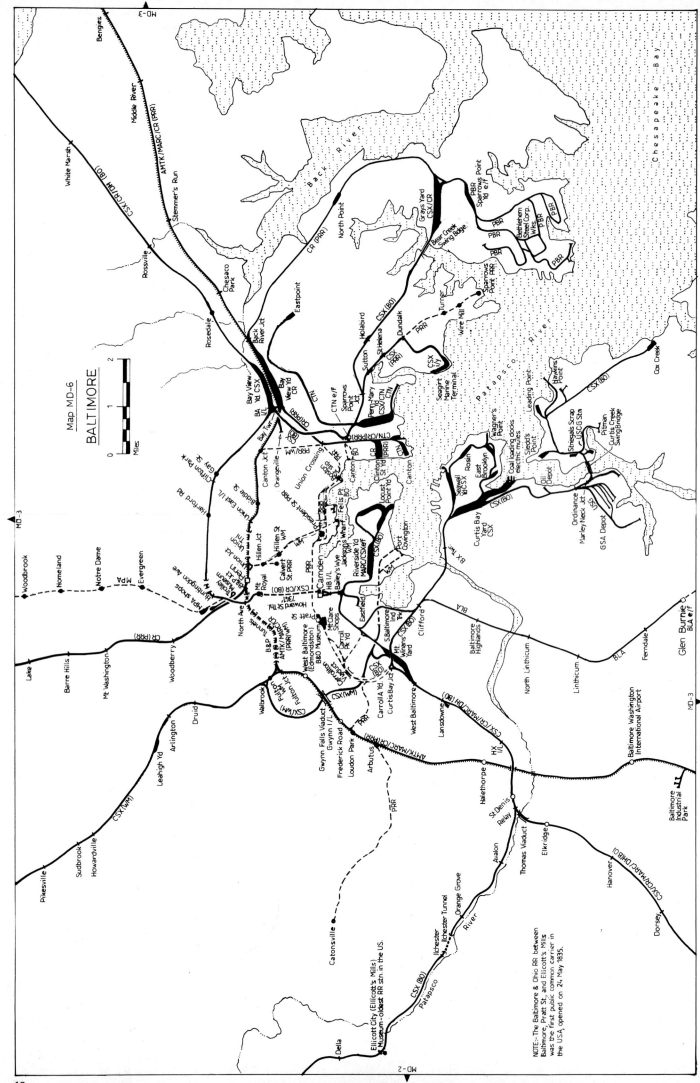

Map MD-6
BALTIMORE

NOTE:- The Baltimore & Ohio RR between Baltimore, Pratt St, and Ellicott's Mills was the first public common carrier in the USA, opened on 24 May 1835.

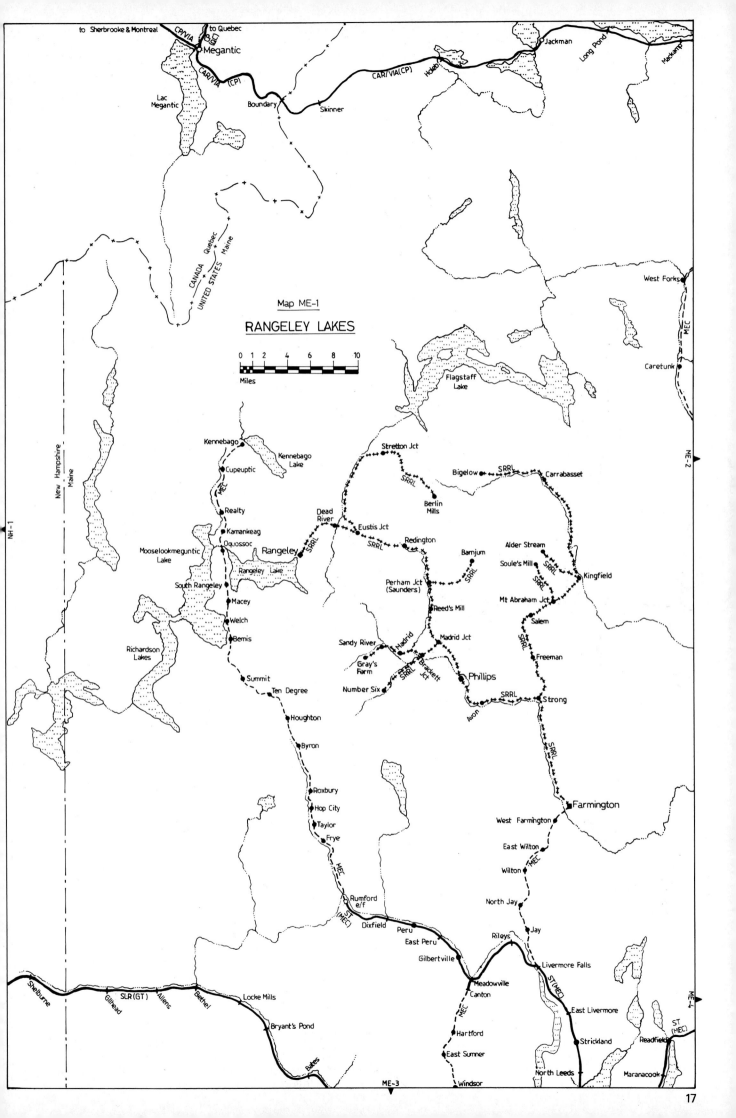

Map ME-1

RANGELEY LAKES

0 1 2 4 6 8 10
Miles

17

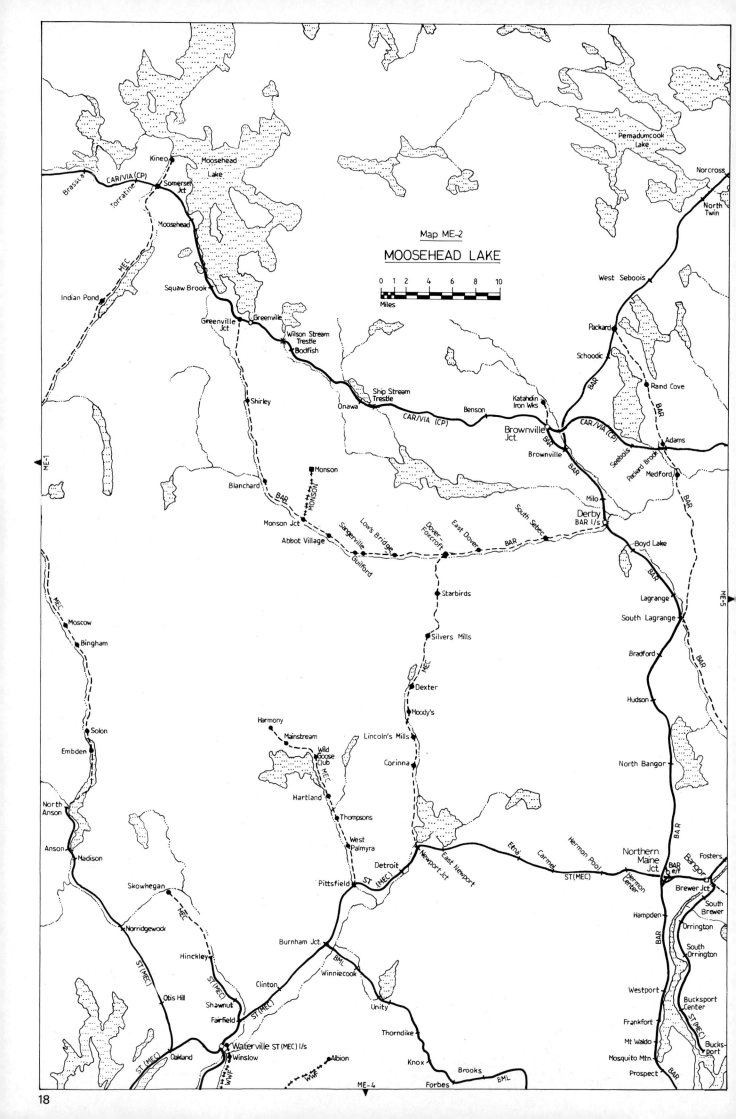

Map ME-2

MOOSEHEAD LAKE

Miles
0 1 2 4   6   8   10

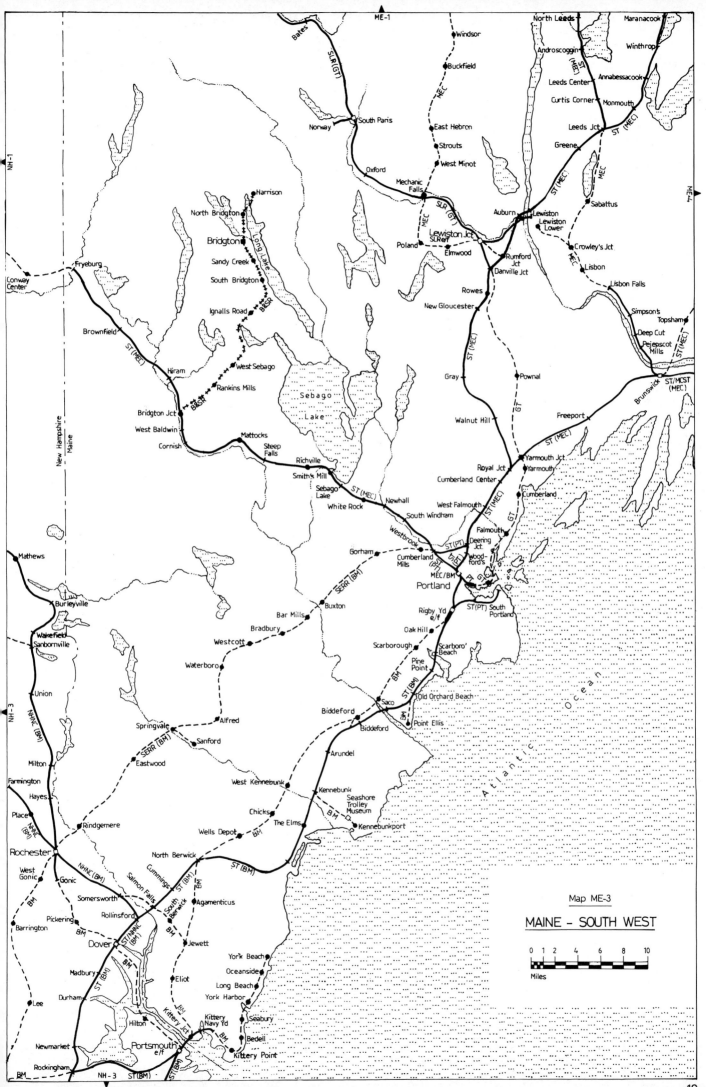

Map ME-3

MAINE - SOUTH WEST

0 1 2 4 6 8 10

Miles

19

CENTRAL MAINE COAST

Map ME-4

Miles
0 1 2   4   6   8   10

20

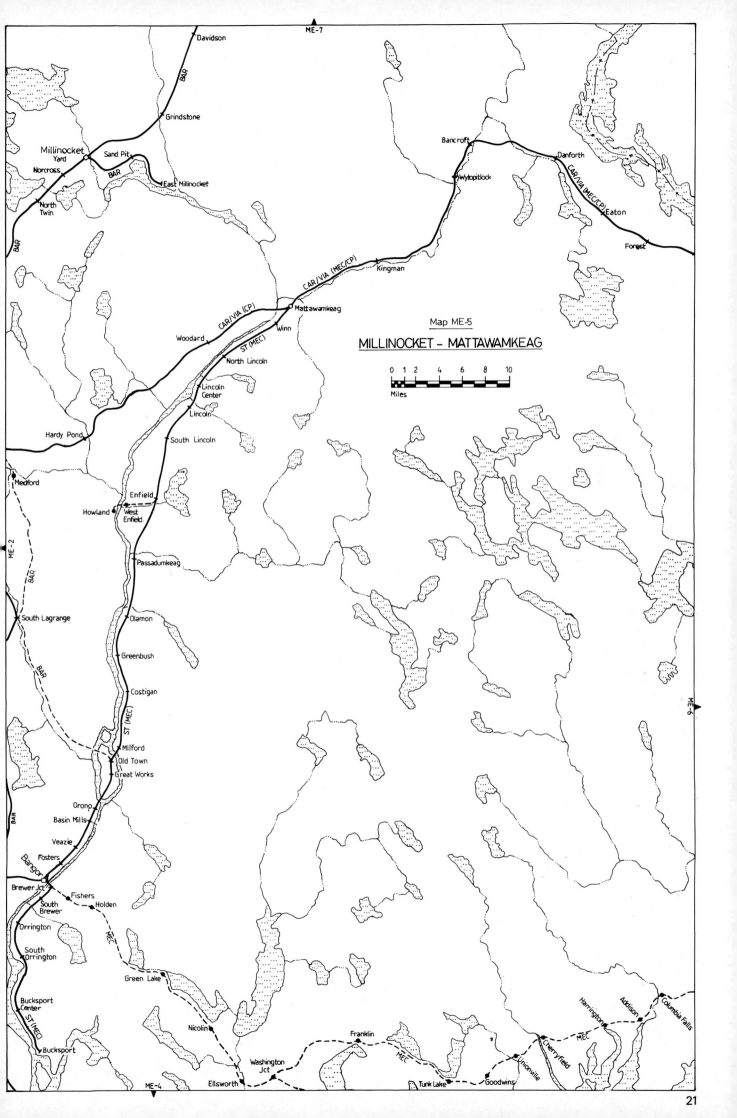

Map ME-5

MILLINOCKET – MATTAWAMKEAG

0 1 2 4 6 8 10
Miles

ME-7

Davidson

BAR

Grindstone

Millinocket
Yard
Norcross   Sand Pit
BAR   East Millinocket
North
Twin

BAR

Bancroft
Wytopitlock   Danforth
CAR/VIA (MEC/CP)
Eaton

Forest

CAR/VIA (MEC/CP)   Kingman

CAR/VIA (CP)
Woodard   Mattawamkeag
ST (MEC)   Winn
North Lincoln
Lincoln
Center
Lincoln
Hardy Pond   South Lincoln

Medford

Howland   Enfield
West
Enfield

ME-2   BAR

South Lagrange   Passadumkeag

BAR   Olamon

Greenbush

Costigan

ST (MEC)

Milford
Old Town
Great Works

Orono
Basin Mills
Veazie
Fosters
Bangor
Brewer Jct
Fishers   Holden
South
Brewer
Orrington   MEC
South
Orrington

Green Lake

Bucksport
Center   Nicolin

ST (MEC)   Franklin

Bucksport   Harrington   Addison   Columbia Falls

Washington
Jct   MEC   Cherryfield
Unionville
ME-4   Ellsworth   Tunk Lake   Goodwins   MEC

ME-6

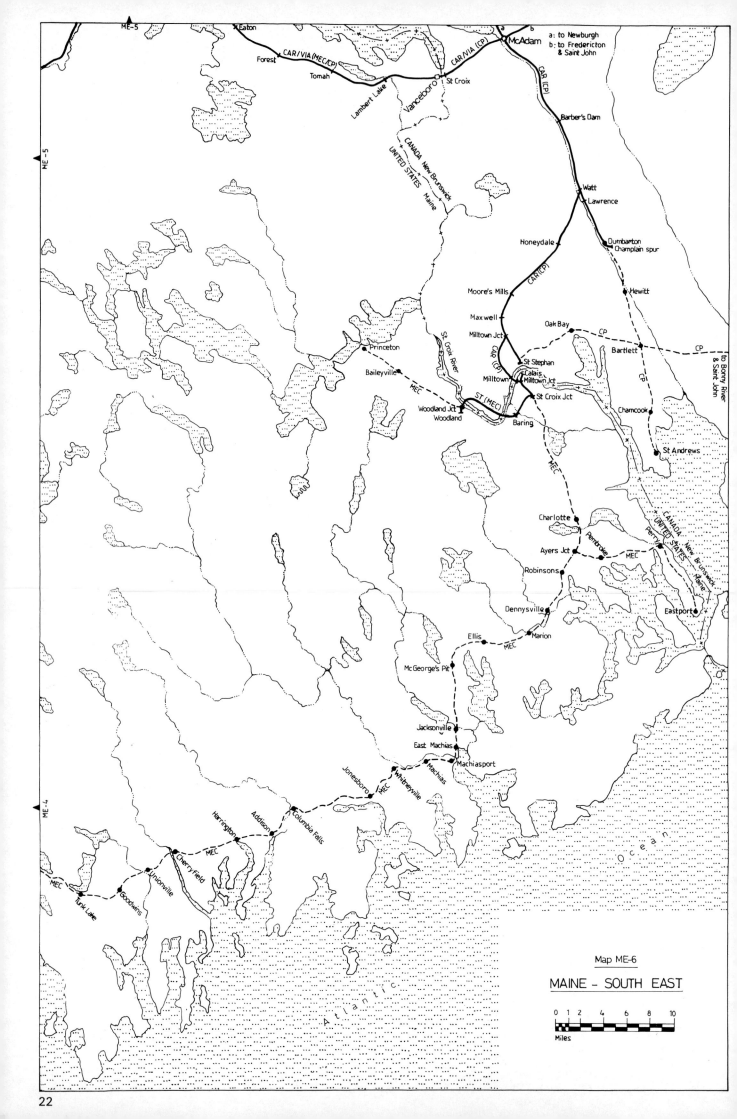

ME-5

Eaton
Forest
CAR/VIA (MEC/CP)
Tomah
Lambert Lake
Vanceboro
St Croix
CAR/VIA (CP)

McAdam
a: to Newburgh
b: to Fredericton & Saint John
CAR (CP)

Barber's Dam

Watt
Lawrence

Honeydale
Dumbarton
Champlain spur

CANADA New Brunswick
UNITED STATES Maine

Moore's Mills
CAR (CP)
Hewitt

Maxwell
Oak Bay
Bartlett
CP
CP

Milltown Jct
CAR (CP)

Princeton
St Stephan
St Croix River
Calais
Milltown Jct
to Bonny River & Saint John

Baileyville
MEC
Milltown
St Croix Jct
Chamcook

Woodland Jct
ST (MEC)
Woodland
Baring
St Andrews

MEC

CANADA New Brunswick
UNITED STATES Maine

Charlotte
Pembroke
Ayers Jct
MEC
Perry

Robinsons
Eastport

Dennysville

Ellis
MEC
Marion

McGeorge's Pit

Jacksonville
East Machias
Machiasport
Jonesboro
Machias
Whitneyville
MEC
Harrington
Addison
Columbia Falls

MEC
Cherryfield
MEC
Unionville
Goodwins
Tunk Lake

ME-4

Atlantic
Ocean

Map ME-6

MAINE – SOUTH EAST

0 1 2 4 6 8 10
Miles

22

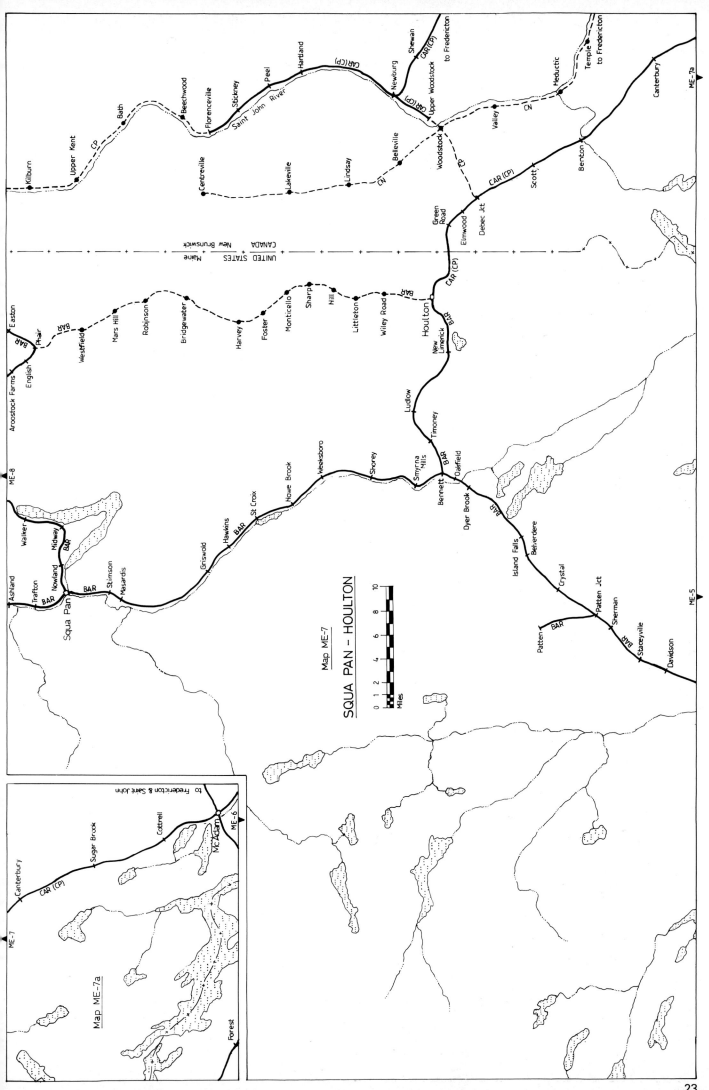

Map ME-7

SQUA PAN – HOULTON

Miles
0 1 2 4 6 8 10

Map ME-7a

UNITED STATES / Maine
CANADA / New Brunswick

Kilburn
Upper Kent
CP
Bath
Beechwood
Florenceville
Centreville
Stickney
Peel
Hartland
CAR (CP)
Saint John River
Lakeville
Lindsay
CN
Belleville
Newburg
Shewan
CAR(CP)
to Fredericton
Upper Woodstock
CAR (CP)
Woodstock
Valley
CN
Heductic
Temple
to Fredericton
Canterbury
ME-7a

Green Road
Elmwood
Debec Jct
Scott,
Benton
CAR (CP)
CAR (CP)

Easton
Phair
BAR
Westfield
Mars Hill
Robinson
Bridgewater
Harvey
Foster
Monticello
Sharpe
Hill
Littleton
Wiley Road
BAR
Houlton
CAR (CP)
BAR
New Limerick

Aroostock Farms
English
BAR
ME-8

Ludlow
Timoney

Walker
Midway
BAR
Griswold
Hawkins
BAR
St Croix
Howe Brook
Weeksboro
Shorey
Smyrna Mills
BAR
Oakfield

Ashland
Trafton
BAR
Newland
Squa Pan
BAR
Stimson
Masardis
Bennett
Dyer Brook
BAR

Island Falls
Belverdere
Crystal
Patten Jct

Patten
BAR
Sherman
BAR
Staceyville
Davidson
ME-5

ME-6
McAdam
to Fredericton & Saint John
Cottrell
Sugar Brook
CAR (CP)
Canterbury
ME-7
Forest

23

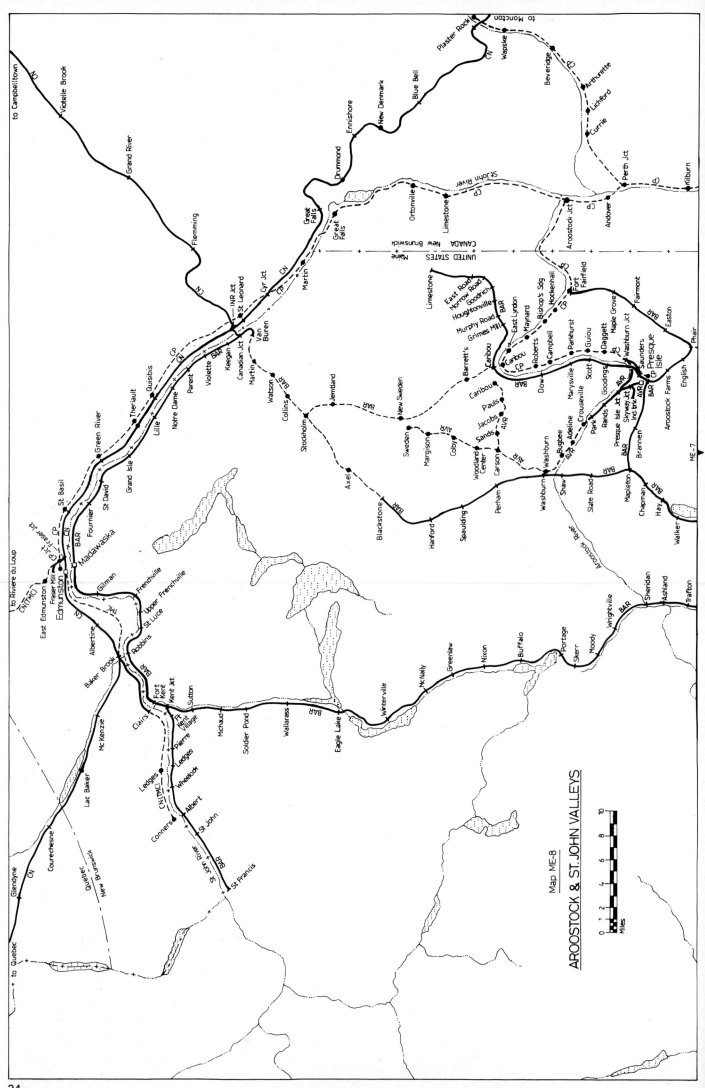

Map ME-8

AROOSTOCK & ST. JOHN VALLEYS

24

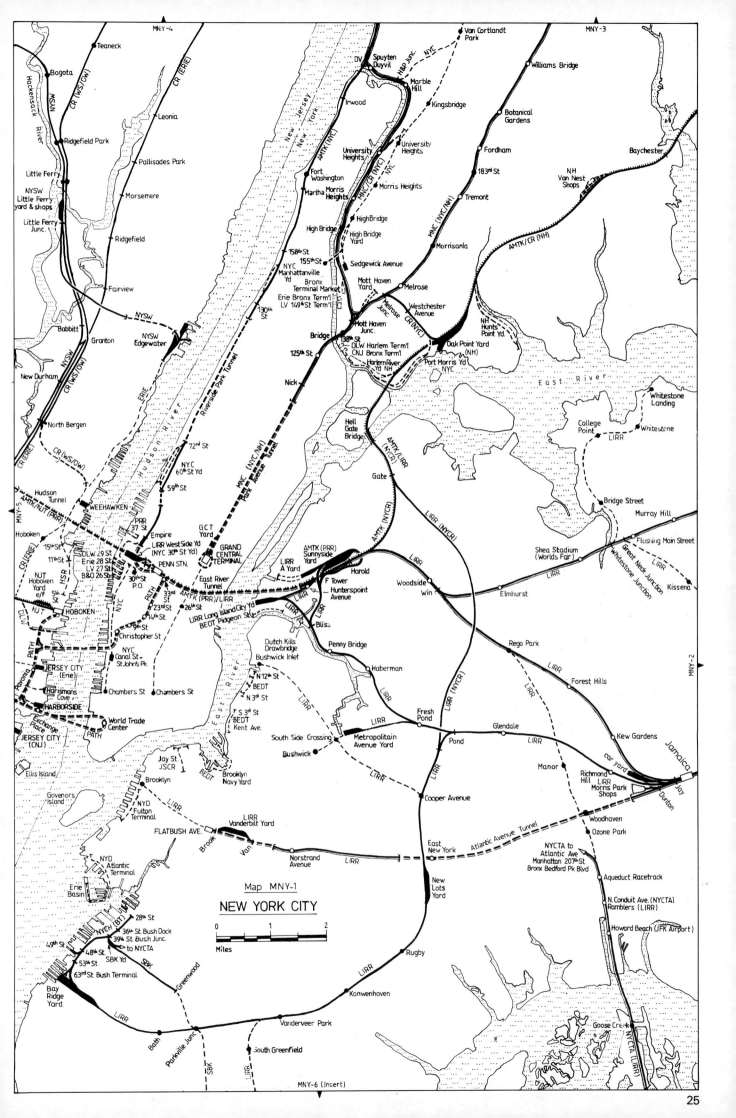

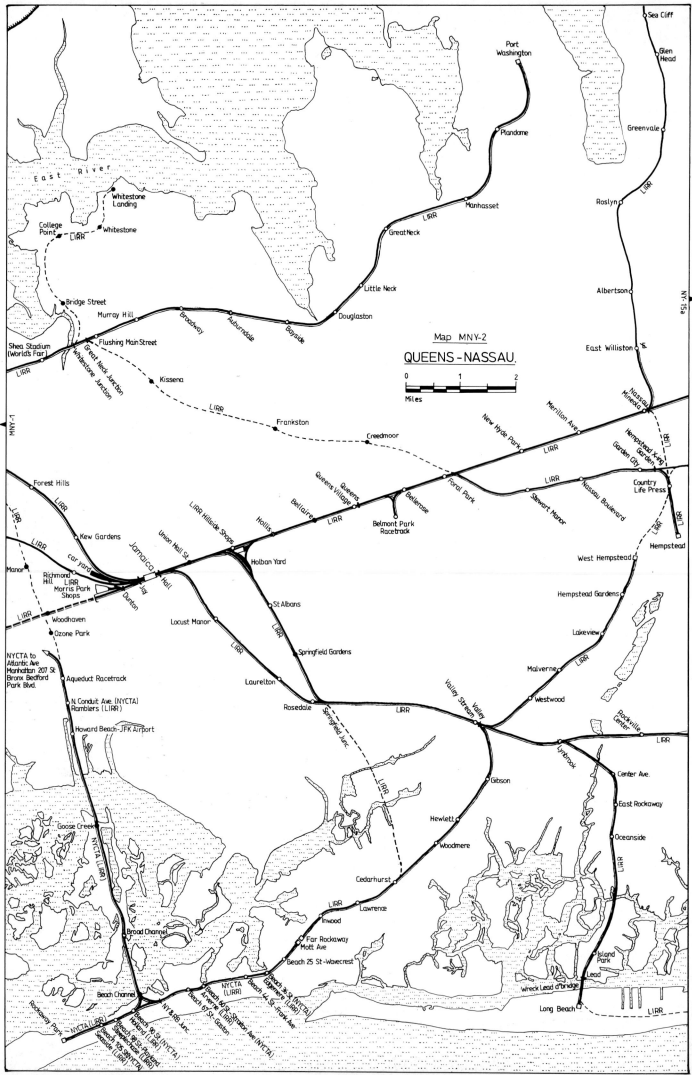

Map MNY-2

QUEENS - NASSAU.

0   1   2
Miles

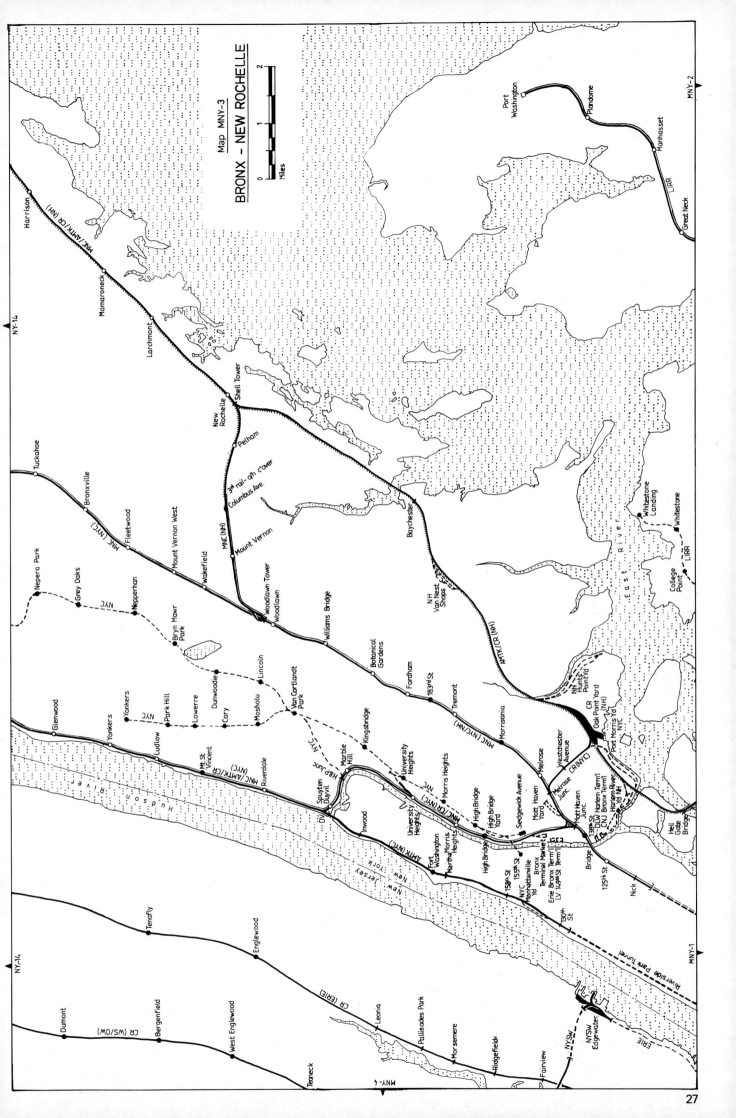

Map MNY-3
BRONX - NEW ROCHELLE

Miles
0   1   2

27

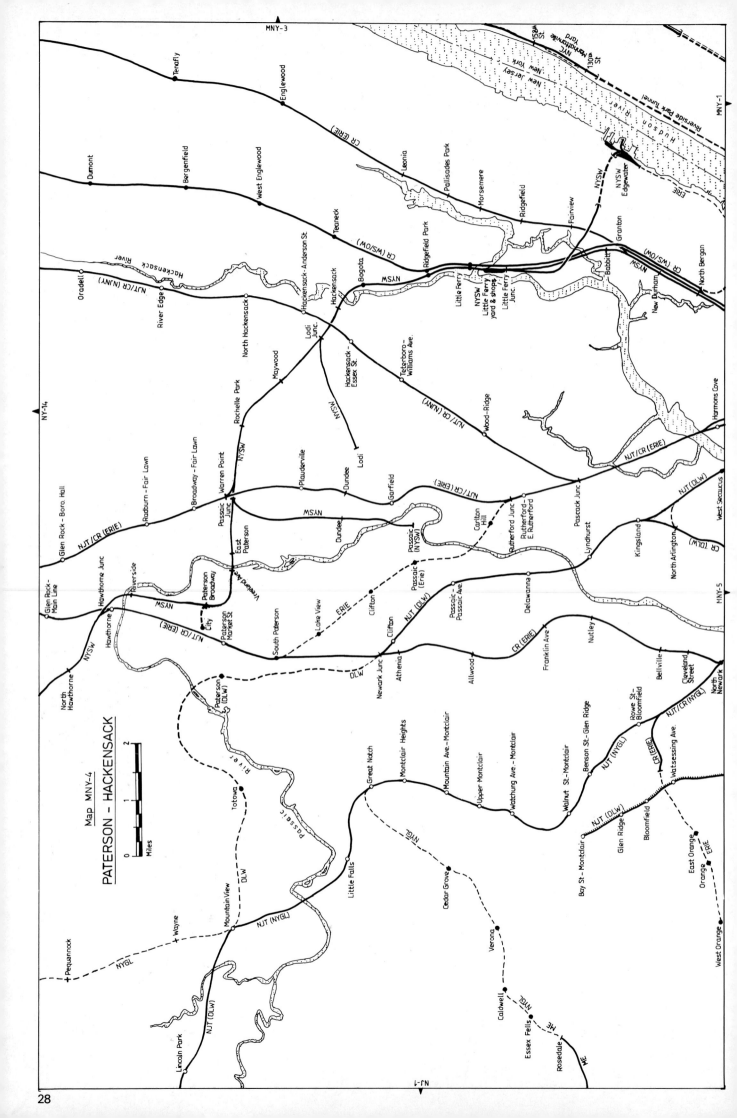

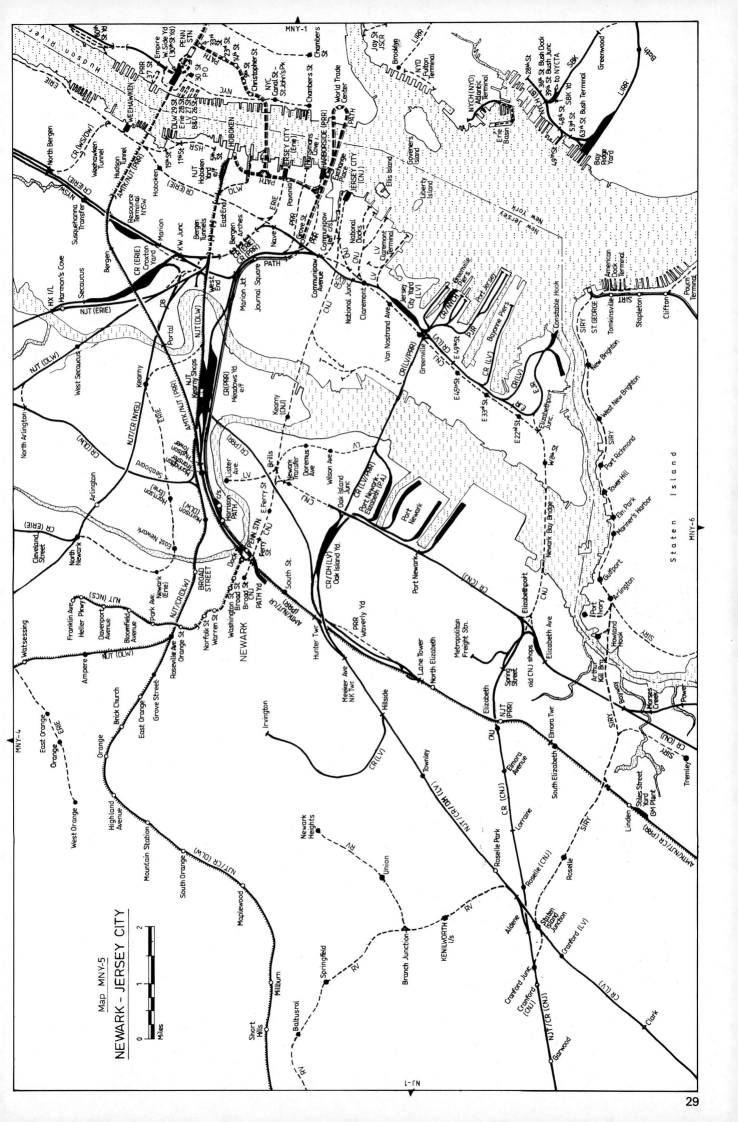

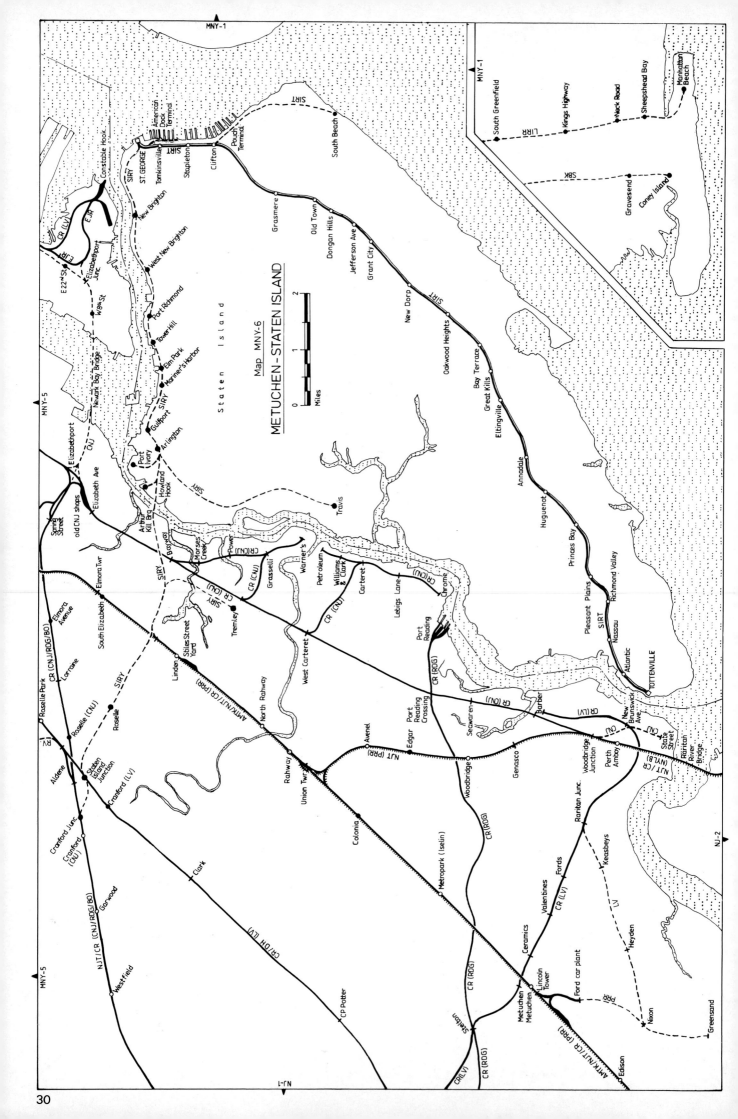

Map MNY-6
METUCHEN – STATEN ISLAND

Staten Island

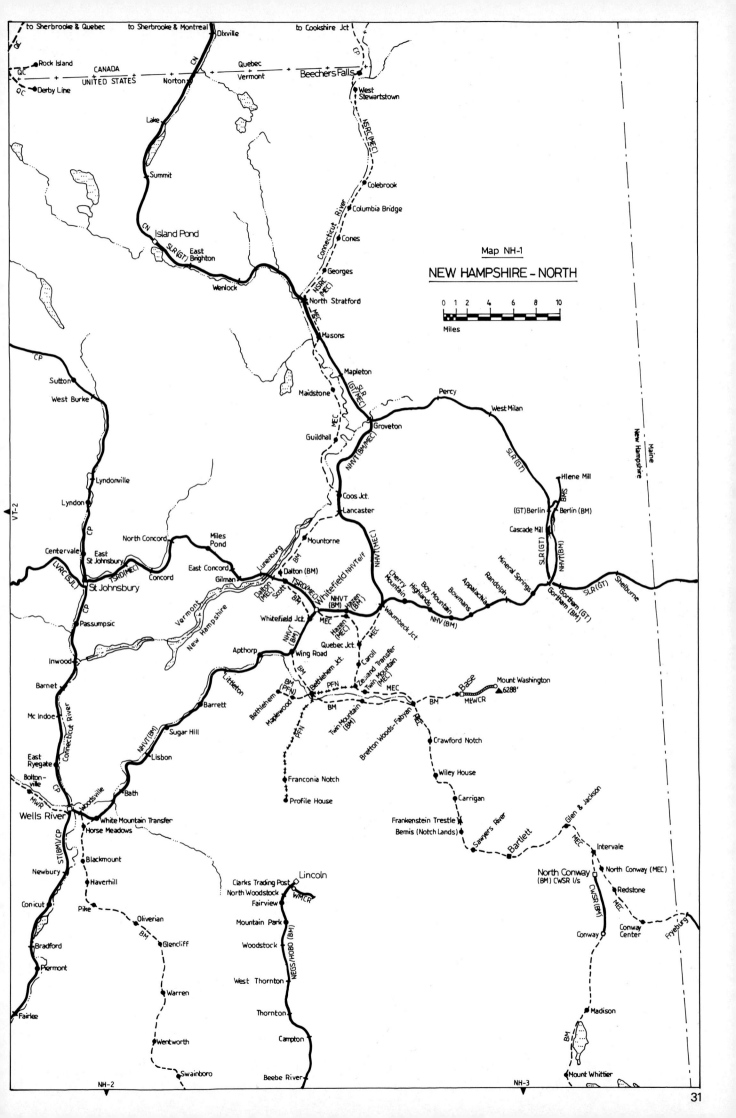

Map NH-1

NEW HAMPSHIRE – NORTH

Miles
0 1 2 4 6 8 10

to Sherbrooke & Quebec to Sherbrooke & Montreal Dixville
to Cookshire Jct

Rock Island
CANADA
UNITED STATES
Norton
Quebec
Vermont
Beechers Falls

Derby Line

West Stewartstown

Lake

Summit

Colebrook

Columbia Bridge

Island Pond
East Brighton
SLR (GT)
CN

Cones

Connecticut River

Georges

Wenlock

NSRC (MEC)
North Stratford

Masons

Sutton
CP

Mapleton

West Milan

Percy

West Burke

Maidstone

SLR (GT/MEC)

MEC

Groveton

Guildhall

Lyndonville

NHVT (BM/MEC)

Coos Jct.

Lancaster

Hlene Mill
BMS

(GT) Berlin Berlin (BM)

Lyndon

Cascade Mill

Centervale
East St Johnsbury
LVRC (S/L)
TSRD (MEC)

North Concord

Miles Pond

Mountorne

NHVT (MEC)

SLR (GT)
NHVT (BM)

St Johnsbury

Concord
East Concord

Lunenburg
Dalton (BM)
BM

Whitefield NHVT e/f
Cherry Mountain
Highlands

Boy Mountain

Bowmans

Appalachia

Randolph

Mineral Springs

Gorham (GT)
Gorham (BM) (GT)
SLR (GT)
Shelburne

Passumpsic

Gilman

Dalton (MEC)
Scott

TSRD (MEC)
BM

Whitefield Jct.

NHVT (BM)
Hazen (BM)

Waumbeck Jct.

NHV (BM)

Vermont
New Hampshire

MEC

Hazen (MEC)

Inwood

Apthorp
NHVT (BM)

Wing Road

Quebec Jct.

Caroll

MEC

Barnet

Connecticut River

Bethlehem Jct.
PFN
Zealand Transfer
Twin Mountain (MEC)

Base
MtWCR

Mount Washington
6288'

Mc Indoe

Littleton

Bethlehem
BM (PFN)
Maplewood

BM

MEC

BM

Barrett

Twin Mountain (BM)

NHVT (BM)
Sugar Hill

Crawford Notch

East Ryegate

Lisbon

PFN

Bretton Woods-Fabyan

Wiley House

Bolton-ville
MWR

Bath

Franconia Notch

Carrigan

Wells River

Woodsville
White Mountain Transfer

Profile House

Frankenstein Trestle

Sawyers River

Bartlett

Glen & Jackson
MEC

Horse Meadows

Bemis (Notch Lands)

Intervale

ST (BM)/CP
CP

Blackmount

Clarks Trading Post
Lincoln
North Woodstock
Fairview
WMCR

North Conway (BM) CWSR I/s

North Conway (MEC)

Newbury

Haverhill

Mountain Park

Redstone

Conicut

Pike

BM

Oliverian

Woodstock

NEGS/HOBO (BM)

CWSR (BM)
MEC

Conway
Conway Center
Fryeburg

Bradford

Glencliff

West Thornton

Piermont

Warren

Thornton

Madison

Fairlee

Wentworth

Campton

BM

Swainboro

Beebe River

Mount Whittier

New Hampshire
Maine

CN

CP

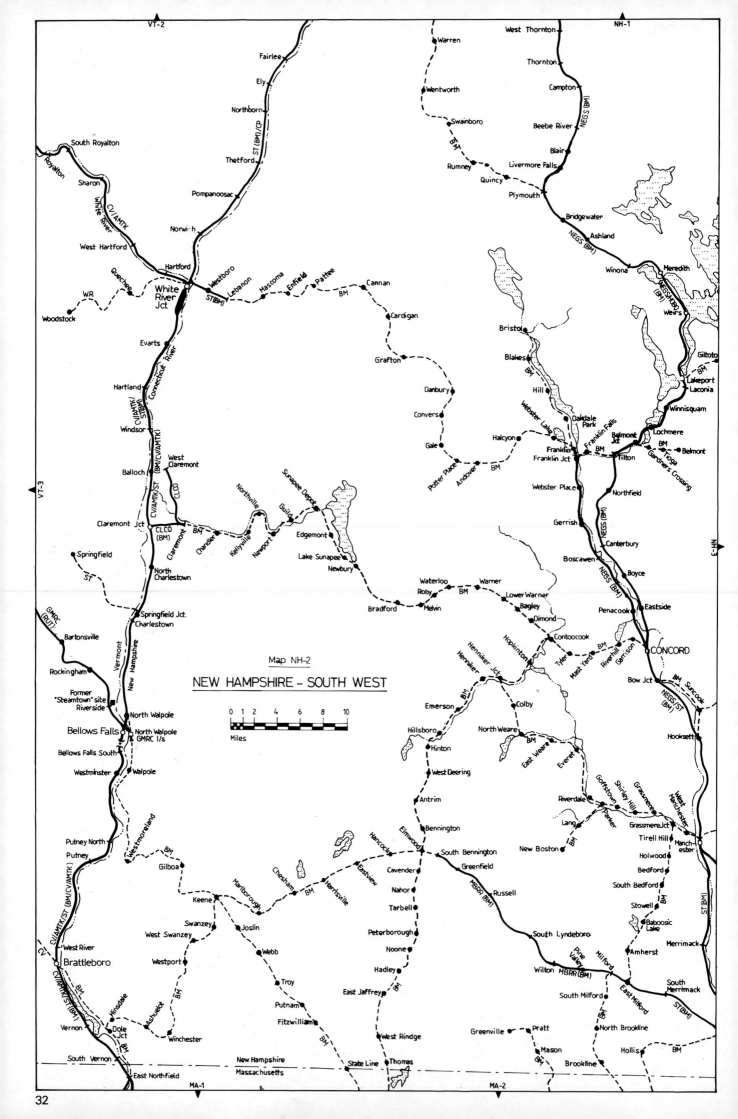

Map NH-2

NEW HAMPSHIRE – SOUTH WEST

0 1 2   4   6   8   10

Miles

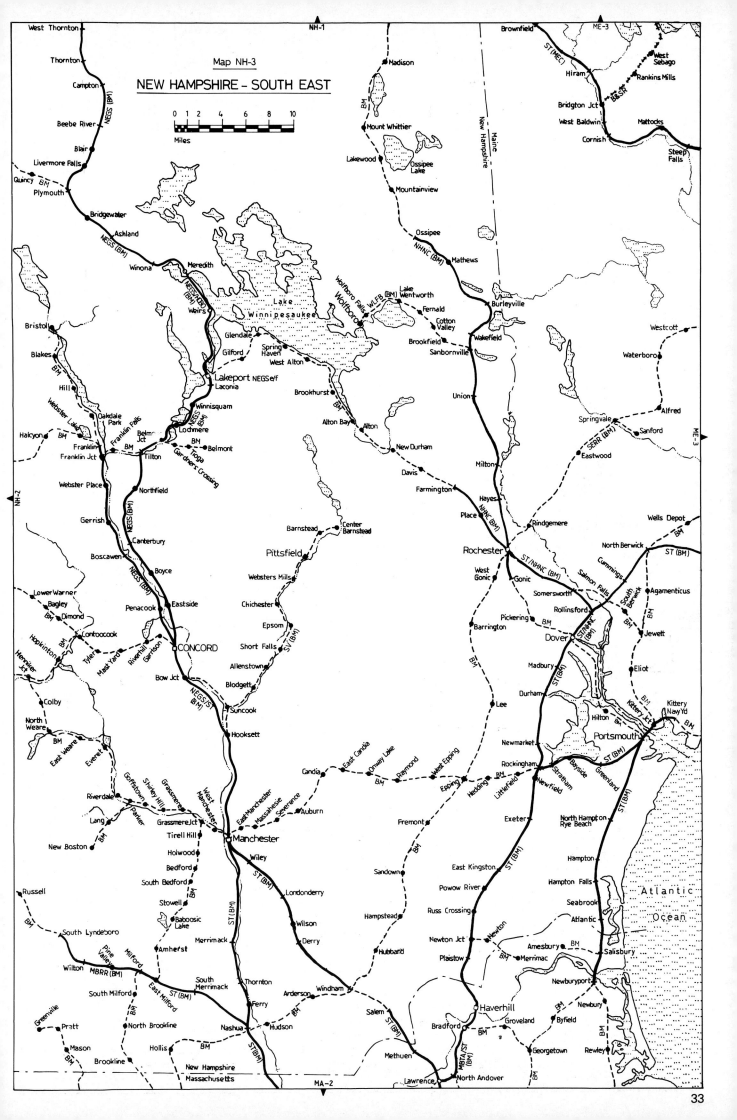

Map NH-3

NEW HAMPSHIRE – SOUTH EAST

0 1 2 4 6 8 10
Miles

West Thornton
Thornton
Campton
Beebe River
Blair
Livermore Falls
Quincy BM
Plymouth
Bridgewater
Ashland
Winona
Bristol
Blakes
Hill
Halcyon
Oakdale Park
Webster Lake
Franklin
Franklin Jct
Webster Place
Gerrish
Boscawen
Boyce
Lower Warner
Bagley
Dimond
Hopkinton
Contoocook
Henniker Jct
Tyler
Colby
North Weare
East Weare
Russell
Riverdale
Lang
New Boston
South Lyndeboro
Pratt
Mason
Greenville
Wilton
South Milford
Pine Valley
MBRR (BM)
Milford
East Milford
South Merrimack
Amherst
Baboosic Lake
Stowell
South Bedford
Bedford
Holwood
Tirell Hill
Grassmere Jct
Goffstown
Shirley Hill
Grassmere
Parker
Riverdale
West Manchester
East Manchester
Massabesic
Auburn
Severence
Wiley
Manchester
Londonderry
Wilson
Derry
Merrimack
Thornton
Anderson
Ferry
Nashua
Hudson
North Brookline
Brookline
Hollis

New Hampshire
Massachusetts
MA-2

Meredith
Weirs
Glendale
Gilford
Spring Haven
West Alton
Lakeport NEGSe/f
Laconia
Winnisquam
Lochmere
Belmont Jct
Franklin Falls
Tilton
Gardners Crossing
Belmont
Tioga
Northfield
Canterbury
Penacook
Eastside
Concord
Rivermill
Garrison
Mast Yard
Bow Jct
Blodgett
Suncook
Hooksett
West Manchester

Lake Winnipesaukee
Wolfboro Falls
Wolfboro
WLFB (BM)
Lake Wentworth
Fernald
Cotton Valley
Brookfield
Sanbornville
Brookhurst
Alton Bay
Alton
New Durham
Davis
Farmington
Barnstead
Center Barnstead
Pittsfield
Websters Mills
Chichester
Epsom
Short Falls
SV (BM)
Allenstown
Lee
Candia
East Candia
Onway Lake
Raymond
West Epping
Fremont
Epping
Hedding
Littlefield
Newfield
Sandown
Hampstead
Hubbard
Salem
Bradford
Methuen
Lawrence

Madison
Mount Whittier
Lakewood
Ossipee Lake
Mountainview
Ossipee
NHNC (BM)
Mathews
Burleyville
Wakefield
Union
Milton
Hayes
Place
NHNC (BM)
Rindgemere
Rochester
West Gonic
Gonic
ST/NHNC (BM)
Somersworth
Barrington
Pickering
Rollinsford
Dover ST/NHNC (BM)
Madbury
Durham
Newmarket
Rockingham
Stratham
Bayside
Newfield
Exeter
North Hampton
Rye Beach
Hampton
Hampton Falls
Seabrook
Atlantic
Newton
Newton Jct
Powow River
East Kingston
Russ Crossing
Plaistow
Amesbury
Merrimac
Newton
Salisbury
Newburyport
Newbury
Byfield
Haverhill
Groveland
Bradford
Georgetown
Rowley

Brownfield
ME-3
Hiram
ST (MEC)
West Sebago
Rankins Mills
Bridgton Jct
West Baldwin
Cornish
Mattocks
Steep Falls
Westcott
Waterboro
Springvale
SERR (BM)
Sanford
Alfred
Eastwood
Wells Depot
North Berwick
Cummings
Salmon Falls
South Berwick
Agamenticus
Jewett
Eliot
Hilton
Kittery Jct
Kittery Navy Yd
Portsmouth
Greenland
Atlantic Ocean

New Hampshire
Maine

NH-1
NH-2
ME-3

NEGS (BM)
NEGS/BM (BM)
NEGS/S (BM)
ST (BM)
BM
BB SR

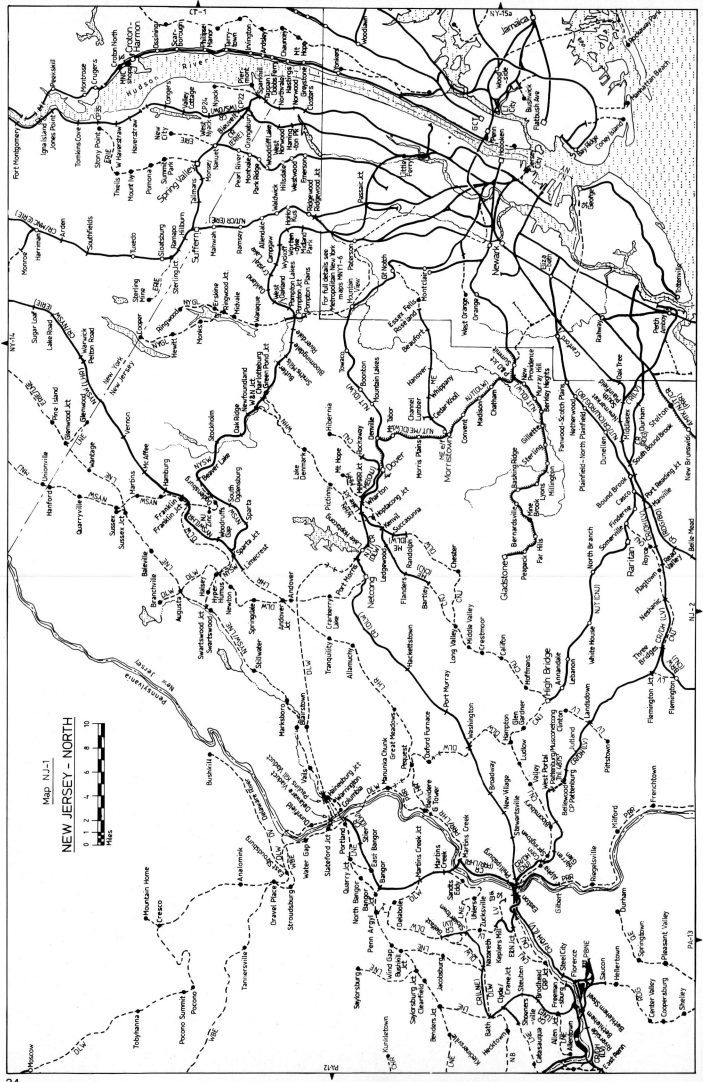

Map NJ-1

NEW JERSEY - NORTH

Miles

0 1 2   4   6   8   10

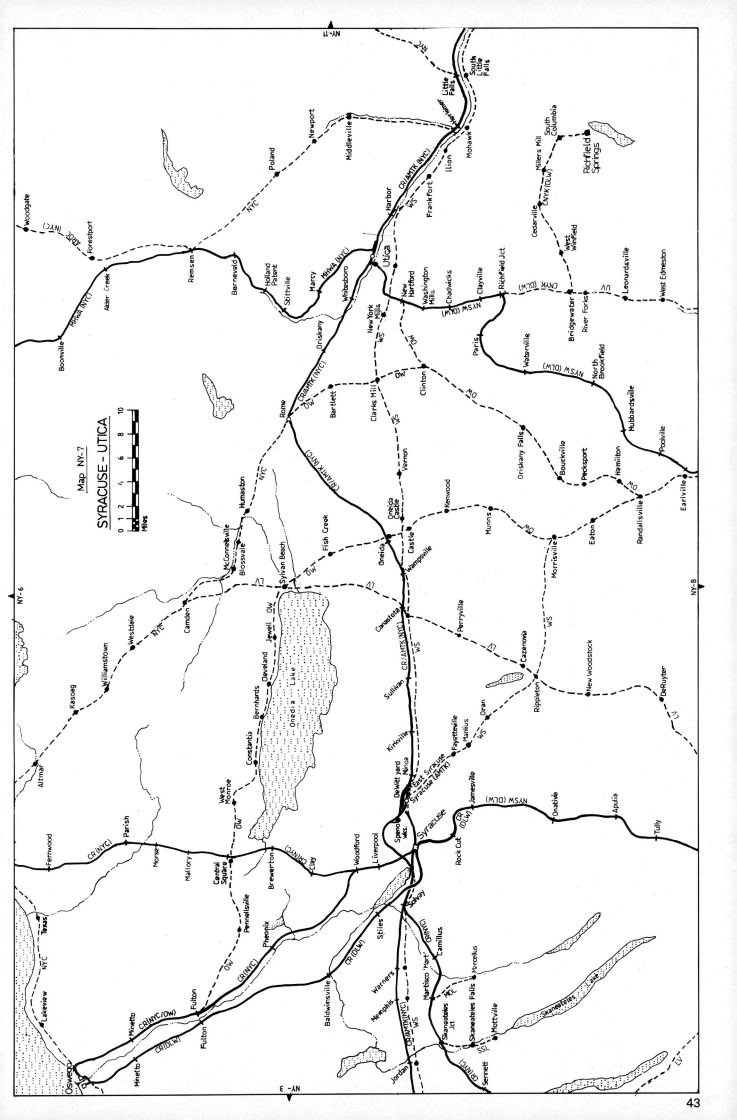

Map NY-7

SYRACUSE - UTICA

Miles
0 1 2 4 6 8 10

43

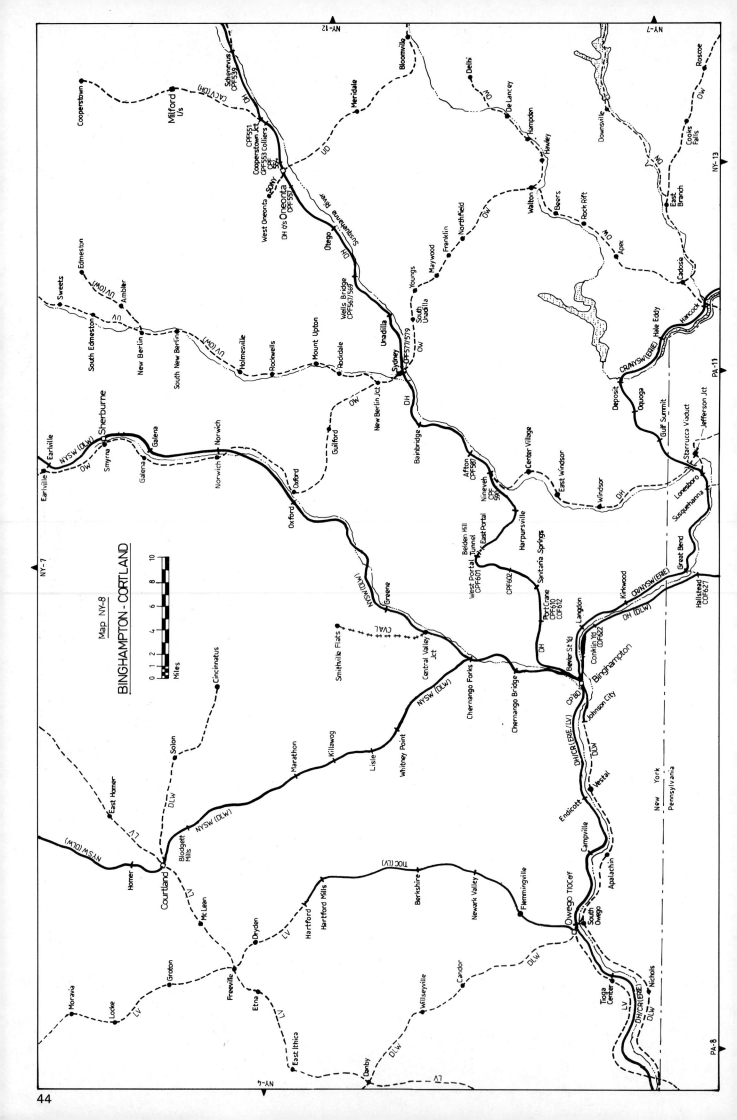

Map NY-8

BINGHAMPTON - CORTLAND

Miles
0 1 2 4 6 8 10

44

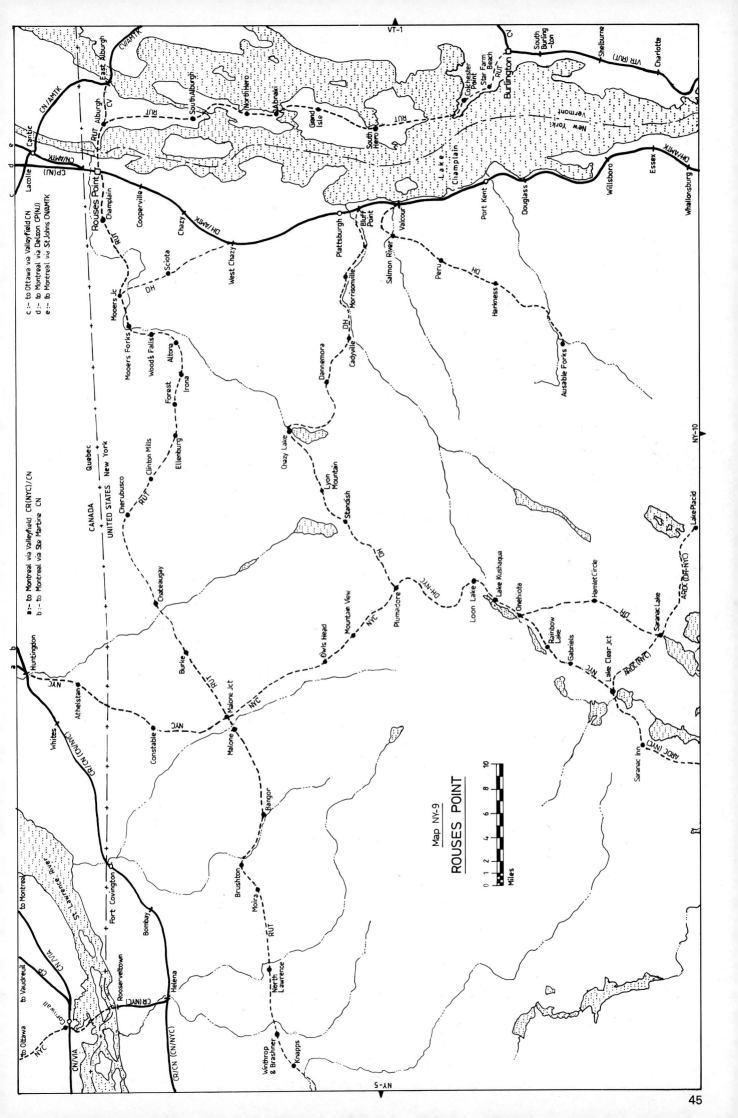

Map NY-9

ROUSES POINT

45

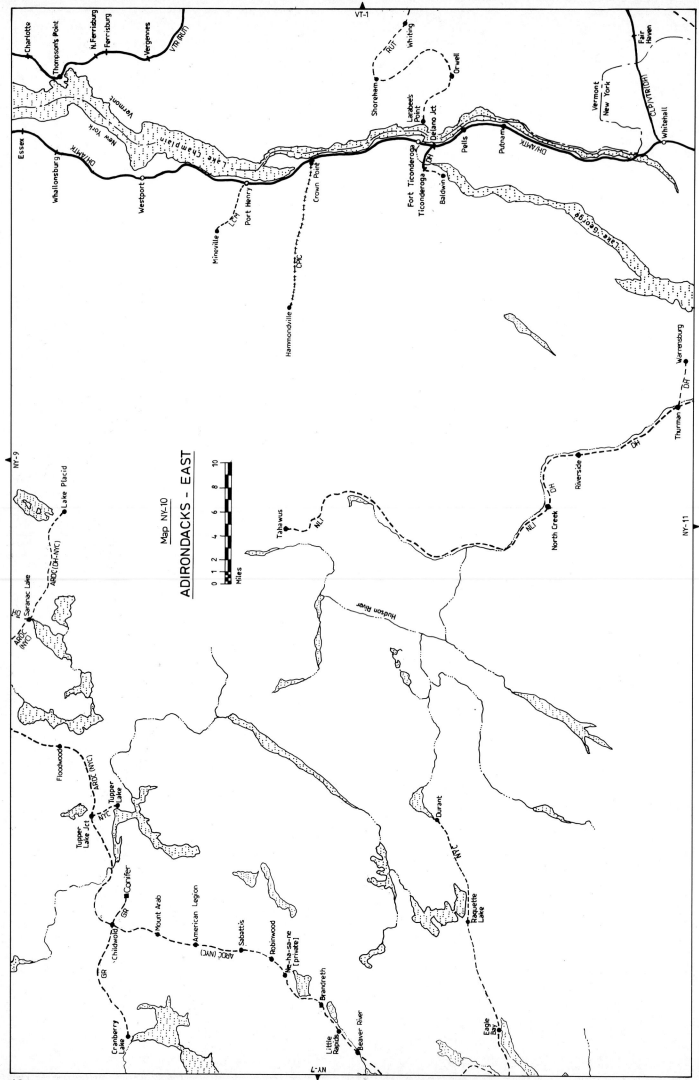

Map NY-10

ADIRONDACKS – EAST

Miles

46

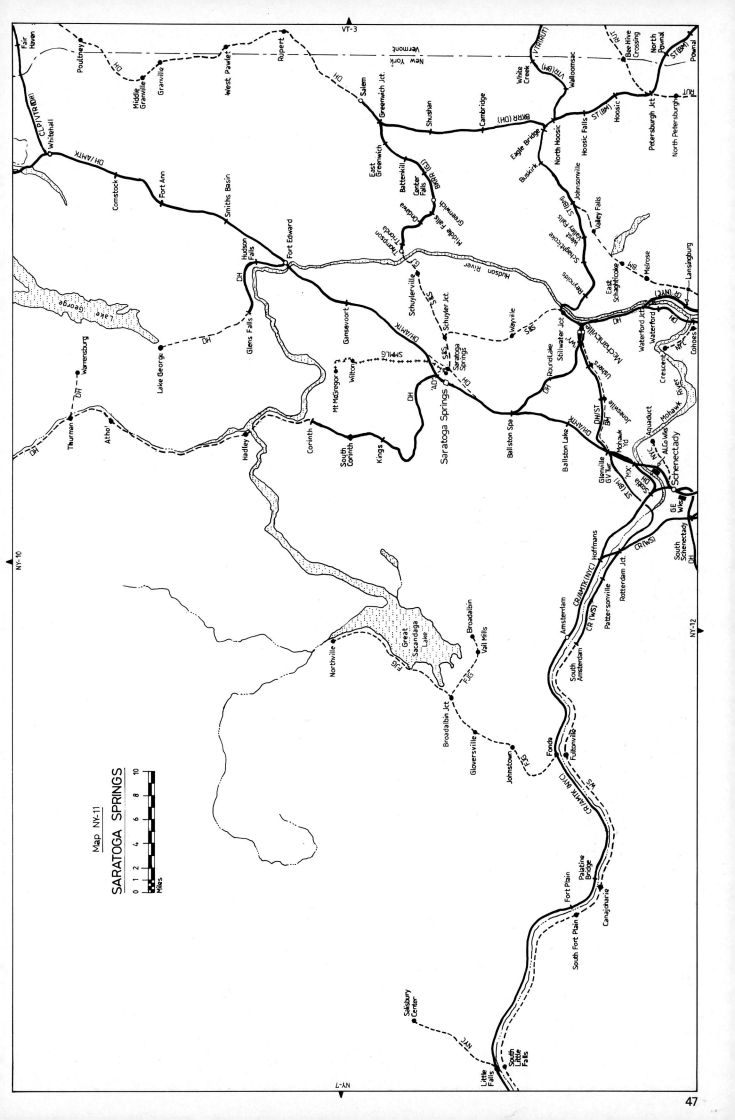

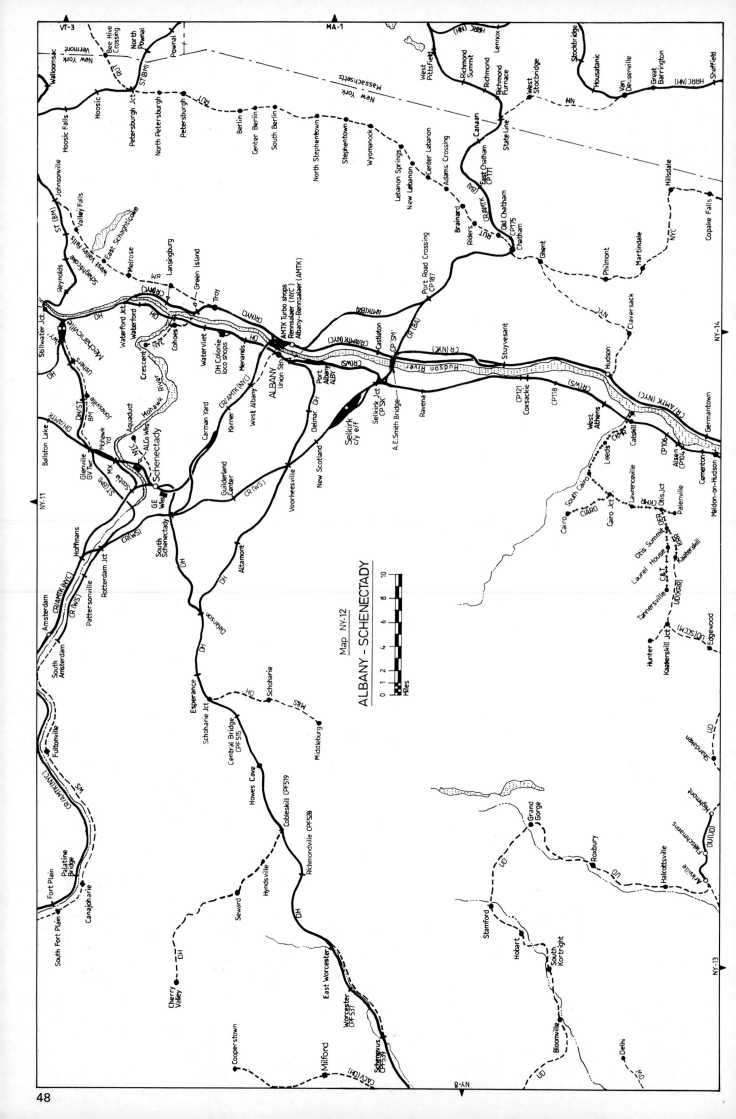

Map NY-12

ALBANY - SCHENECTADY

Miles
0 1 2 4 6 8 10

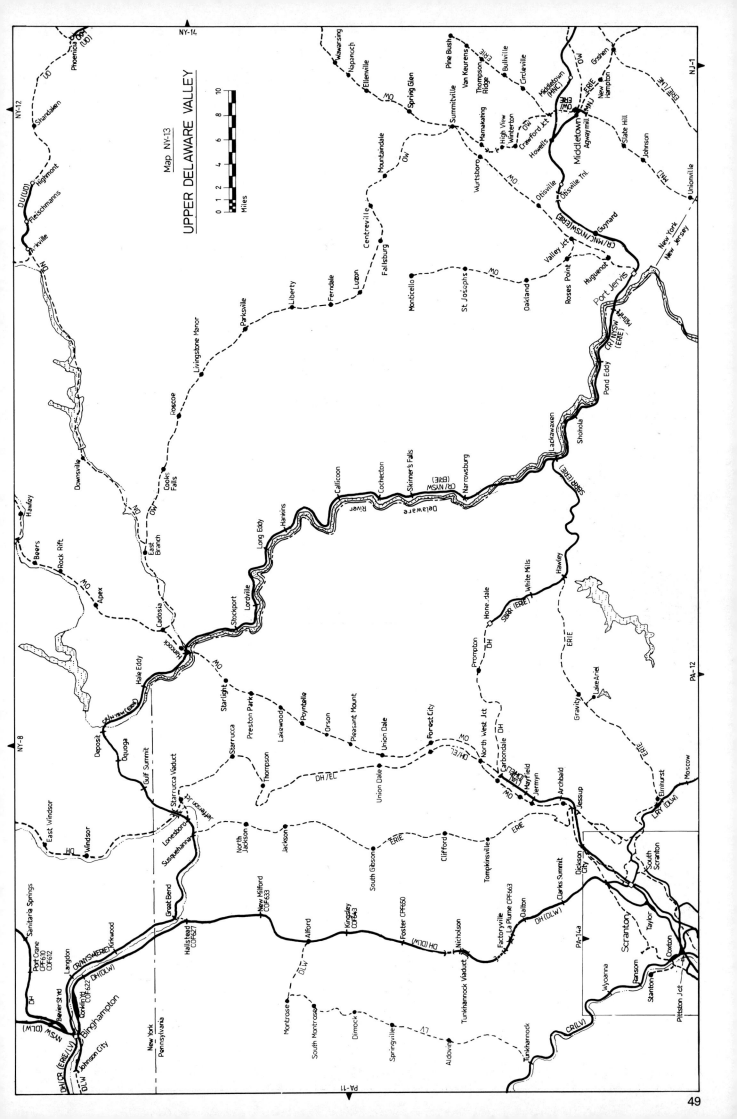

UPPER DELAWARE VALLEY

Map NY-13

0 1 2 4 6 8 10
Miles

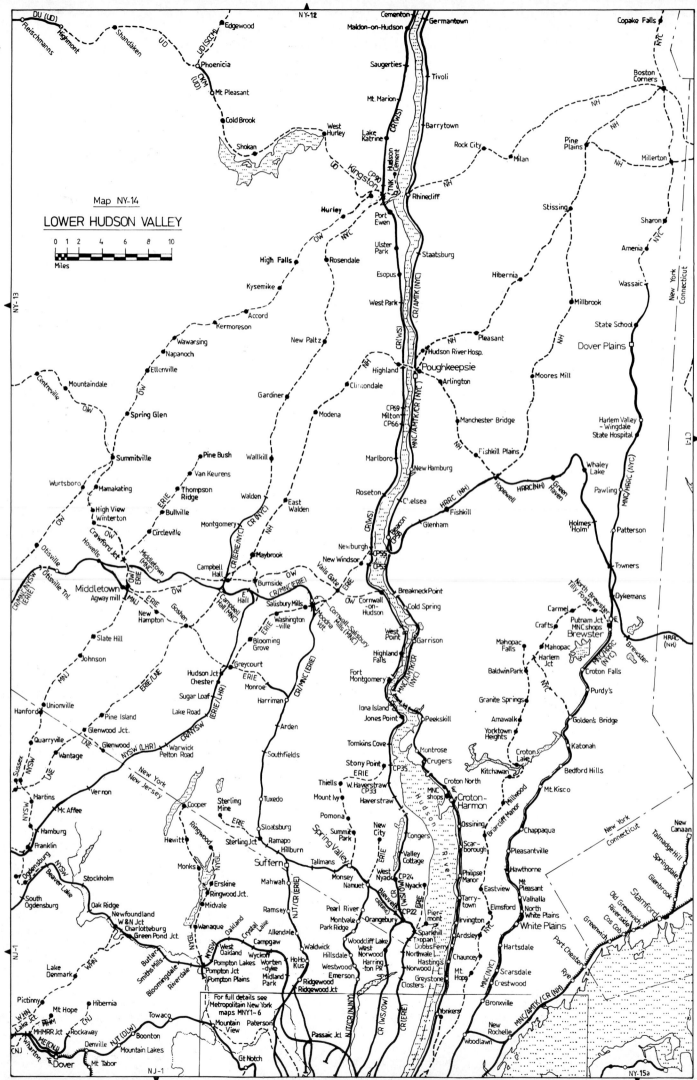

Map NY-14

LOWER HUDSON VALLEY

0 1 2 4 6 8 10
Miles

50

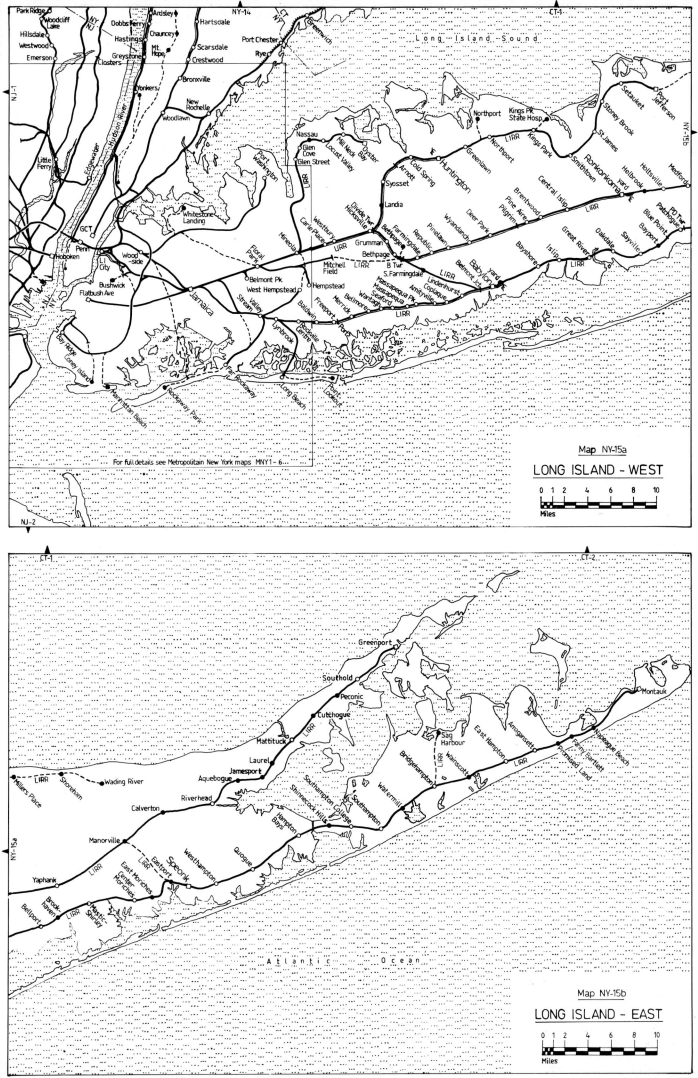

Map NY-15a

LONG ISLAND - WEST

0 1 2 4 6 8 10
Miles

Park Ridge
Woodcliff Lake
Hillsdale
Westwood
Emerson
NY NJ
Little Ferry
Eddewater
Hoboken
GCT
Penn
LI City
Wood-side
Bushwick
Flatbush Ave
Bay Ridge
Coney Island
Manhattan Beach

Dobbs Ferry
Ardsley
Hartsdale
Hastings
Chauncey
Mt. Hope
Greystone
Closters
Yonkers
Bronxville
New Rochelle
Woodlawn
Scarsdale
Crestwood

Hudson River
NJ-1

Whitestone Landing
Jamaica
Rockaway Park

Port Chester
Rye
Greenwich
NY-14
CT-1

Long Island Sound

Nassau
Glen Cove
Glen Street
Port Washington
Locust Valley
Mill Neck Bay
Oyster Bay
LIRR
Westbury
Carle Place
Mineola
Floral Park
Belmont Pk.
West Hempstead
Hempstead
Valley Stream
Baldwin
Freeport
Merrick
Bellmore
Lynbrook
Rockville Centre
Far Rockaway
Long Beach
Point Lookout

Divide Twr
Hicksville
Grumman
Bethpage
Mitchell Field
LIRR
B Twr
S. Farmingdale
Wantagh
Seaford
Massapequa
Massapequa Pk

Cold Spring
Arnott
Syosset
Landia
Farmingdale
Republic
Pinelawn
LIRR
Lindenhurst
Amityville
Copiague

Northport
Kings Pk State Hosp
Northport
Greenlawn
Huntington
Wyandanch
Deer Park
Pine Aire
Pilgrim
Brentwood
Central Islip
Bayshore
Islip
Belmont Jct.
Babylon
yard

Setauket
Port Jefferson
Stoney Brook
St James
Smithtown
Ronkonkoma
yard
Holbrook
Holtsville
Medford
Great River
Oakdale
Sayville
Blue Point
Bayport
Patchogue
PD Twr
LIRR
NY-15b

For full details see Metropolitain New York maps MNY1 - 6

NJ-2

Map NY-15b

LONG ISLAND - EAST

0 1 2 4 6 8 10
Miles

CT-1
CT-2

Greenport
Southold
Peconic
Cutchogue
Mattituck
Laurel
Jamesport
Aquebogue
LIRR
Sag Harbour
East Hampton
Amagansett
Bridgehampton
Wainscott
Watermill
Southampton
Southampton College
Shinnecock Hills
Hampton Bays
Riverhead
Calverton
Manorville
Yaphank
Brook-haven
Bellport
Mastic Shirley
East Moriches
Center Moriches
Eastport
Speonk
Westhampton
Quogue
LIRR
Millers Place
Shoreham
Wading River
LIRR
NY-15a

Montauk
Fanny Bartlett
Promised Land
Napeague Beach
LIRR

Atlantic Ocean

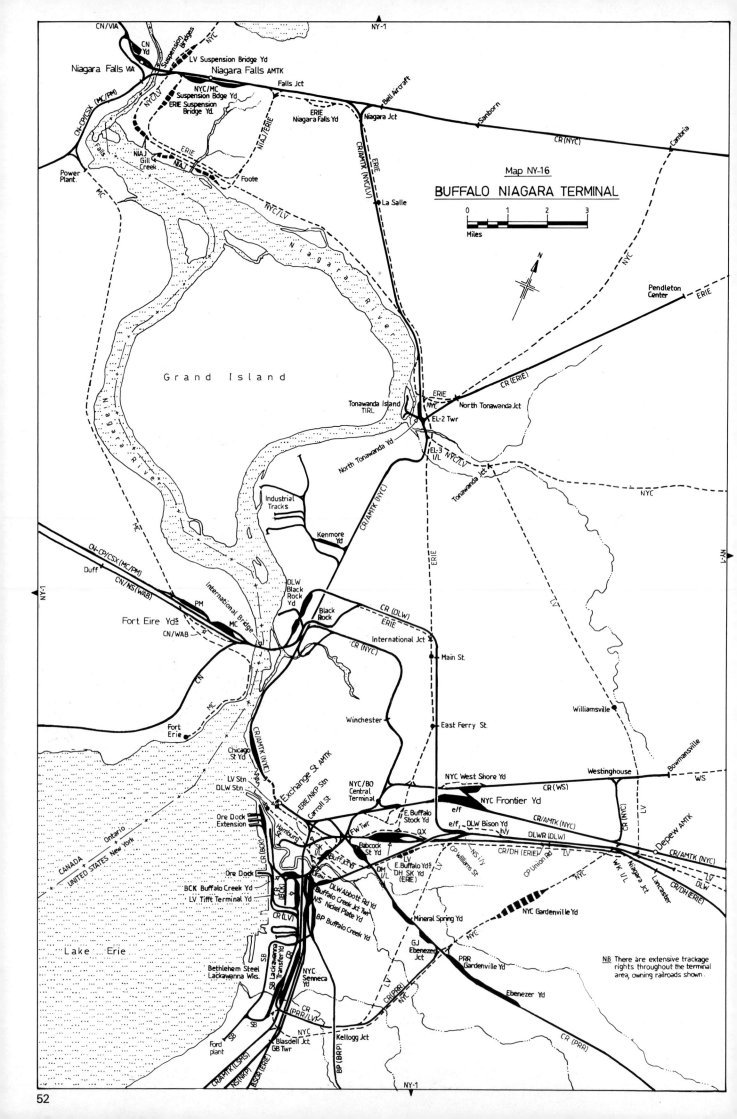

Map NY-16

BUFFALO NIAGARA TERMINAL

0   1   2   3
Miles

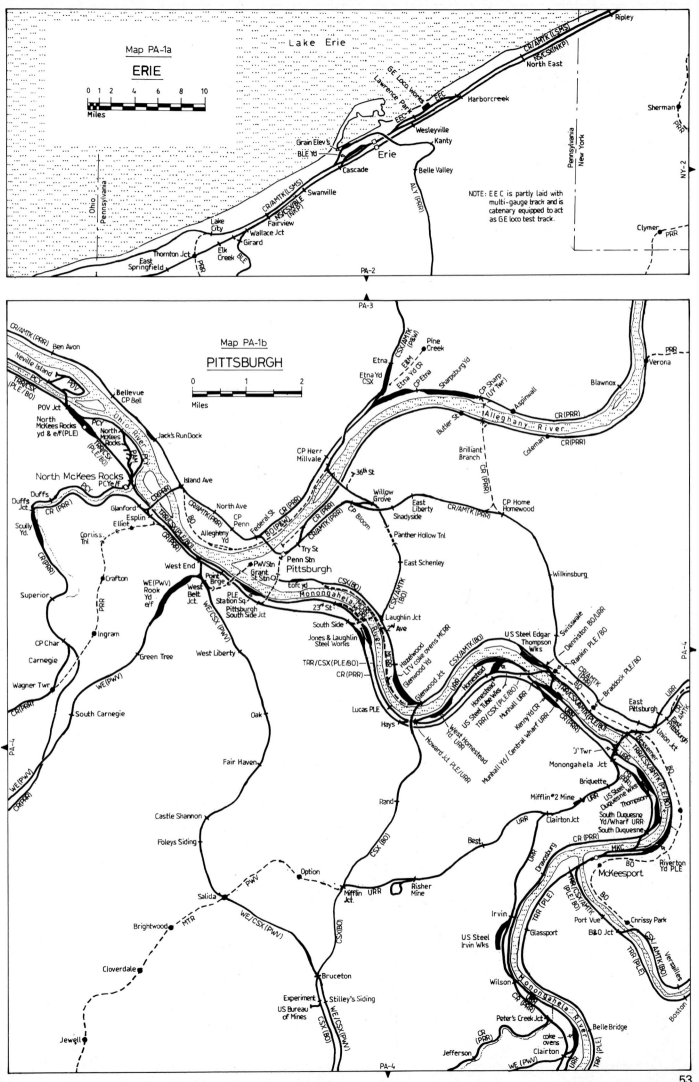

Map PA-1a
ERIE

Miles
0 1 2 4 6 8 10

NOTE: E E C is partly laid with
multi-gauge track and is
catenary equipped to act
as GE loco test track.

Lake Erie

Ripley
CR/AMTK (LSMS)
NS/CSX(NKP)
North East
Sherman
Harborcreek
GE Loco Works
Lawrence Park
EEC
Wesleyville
Kanty
EEC
Grain Elev's
BLE Yd
Erie
Cascade
Belle Valley
ALY (PRR)
CR/AMTK (LSMS)
NS/CSX (NKP)
Swanville
Fairview
Lake City
Wallace Jct
Girard
BLE
Elk Creek
Thornton Jct
East Springfield
PRR
Ohio Pennsylvania
Pennsylvania New York
Clymer PRR
NY-2

PA-2

Map PA-1b
PITTSBURGH

Miles
0 1 2

PA-3

Ben Avon
CR/AMTK (PRR)
Neville Island
POV
POV Jct
North McKees Rocks yd & e/f (PLE)
TRR (CSX) (PLE/BO)
Bellevue CP Bell
PCY
North McKees Rocks
PCY (S)
PLE/BO
PAH
North McKees Rocks
PCY e/f
Jack's Run Dock
Ohio River Duffs
CR (PRR)
Duffs Jct
Glanford
Esplin
Elliot
Scully Yd.
Corliss Tnl
CR (PRR)
CR (PRR)
TRR (CSX) (PLE/BO)
CR (PRR)
Island Ave
North Ave
CP Penn
Allegheny Yd
Superior
Crafton
PRR
West End
WE (PWV) Rook Yd e/f
West Belt Jct.
Point Brge
West End
Federal St
BO (PWV)
CR/AMTK (PRR)
Try St
Penn Stn
Grant St Stn
PwV Stn
Pittsburgh
CP Herr
Millvale
36th St
Willow Grove
East Liberty
Shadyside
CR/AMTK (PRR)
CP Bloom
Panther Hollow Tnl
East Schenley
CR (PRR)
CP Home Homewood
Etna
CSX/AMTK (P&W)
Pine Creek
E&M
Etna Yd CSX
Etna Yd CR
CP Etna
Sharpsburg Yd
CP Sharp (UY Twr)
Aspinwall
Butler St
Brilliant Branch
CR (PRR)
Coleman
CR (PRR)
Allegheny River
Blawnox
Verona
PRR
Wilkinsburg
Ingram
CP Char
Carnegie
Wagner Twr
CR (PRR)
South Carnegie
Green Tree
West Liberty
Oak
Fair Haven
Point St Stn
PLE Station Sq
Pittsburgh South Side Jct
23rd St
South Side
Jones & Laughlin Steel Works
TRR/CSX (PLE/BO)
CR (PRR)
Monongahela River
Eof cyd
CSX (BO)
2nd Ave
Laughlin Jct
CSX/AMTK (BO)
Hazelwood
LTV coke ovens MCRR
Glenwood Yd
Glenwood Jct
Lucas PLE
Hays
Howard Jct PLE/URR
West Homestead
US Steel Tube Wks
Homestead
Homestead
URR
US Steel Edgar Thompson Wks
Swissvale
Denniston BO/URR
Rankin PLE/BO
CR/AMTK
BO
Braddock PLE/BO
East Pittsburgh
Munhall URR
TRR/CSX (PLE/BO)
Munhall Yd/Central Wharf URR
Kenny Yd CR
CR (PRR)
'J' Twr
Monongahela Jct
Briquette
Mifflin #2 Mine
US Steel Duquesne Wks
Thompson
South Duquesne Yd/Wharf URR
South Duquesne
Union Jct
East Pittsburgh
Bessemer
TRR/CSX/AMTK (PLE/BO)
BO
BO
URR
URR
Castle Shannon
Foleys Siding
Rand
Best
CSX (BO)
Clairton Jct
CR (PRR)
Drakusburg
MKC
McKeesport
Riverton Yd PLE
Option
Mifflin Jct
URR
Risher Mine
Salida
WE/CSX (PWV)
Brightwood
MTR
Cloverdale
Bruceton
CSX (BO)
Experiment
US Bureau of Mines
Stilley's Siding
WE/CSX (PWV)
Jewell
US Steel Irvin Wks
Irvin
TRR (PLE)
Glassport
Wilson
Port Vue
Chrissy Park
B&O Jct
CSX/AMTK (BO)
Versailles
TRR (PLE)
Boston
CR (PRR)
Peter's Creek Jct
Belle Bridge
Jefferson
WE (PWV)
coke ovens
Clairton
URR
TRR (PLE)
Monongahela River

PA-4

PA-4

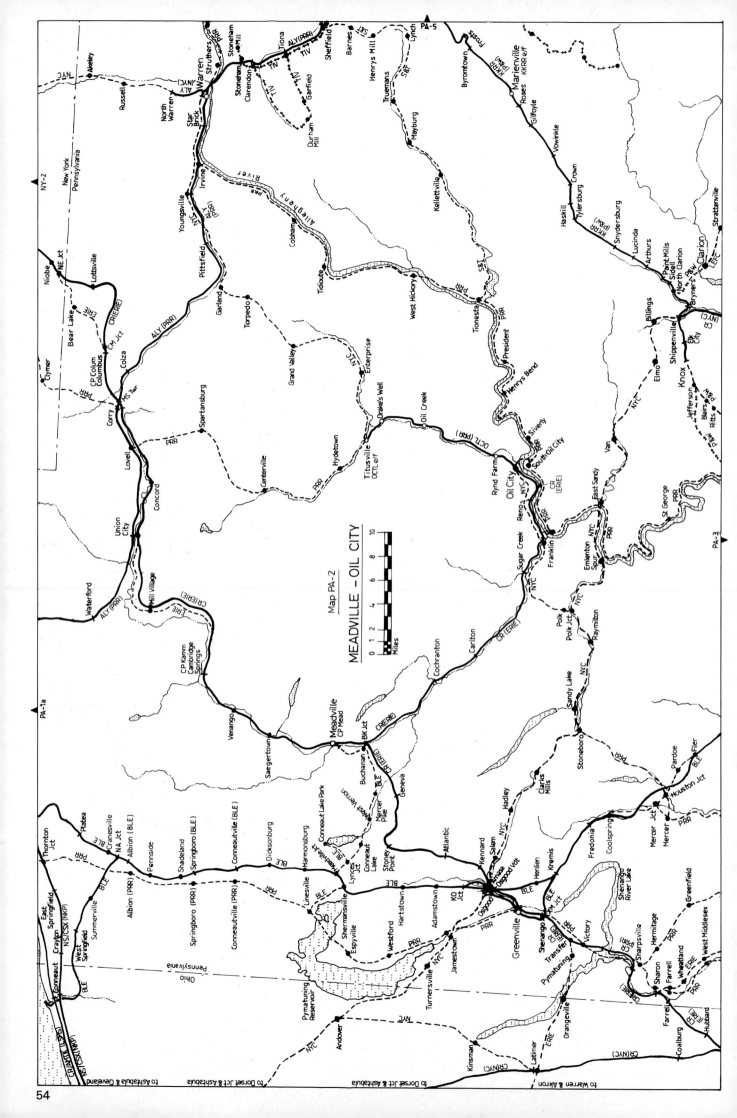

Map PA-2

MEADVILLE – OIL CITY

54

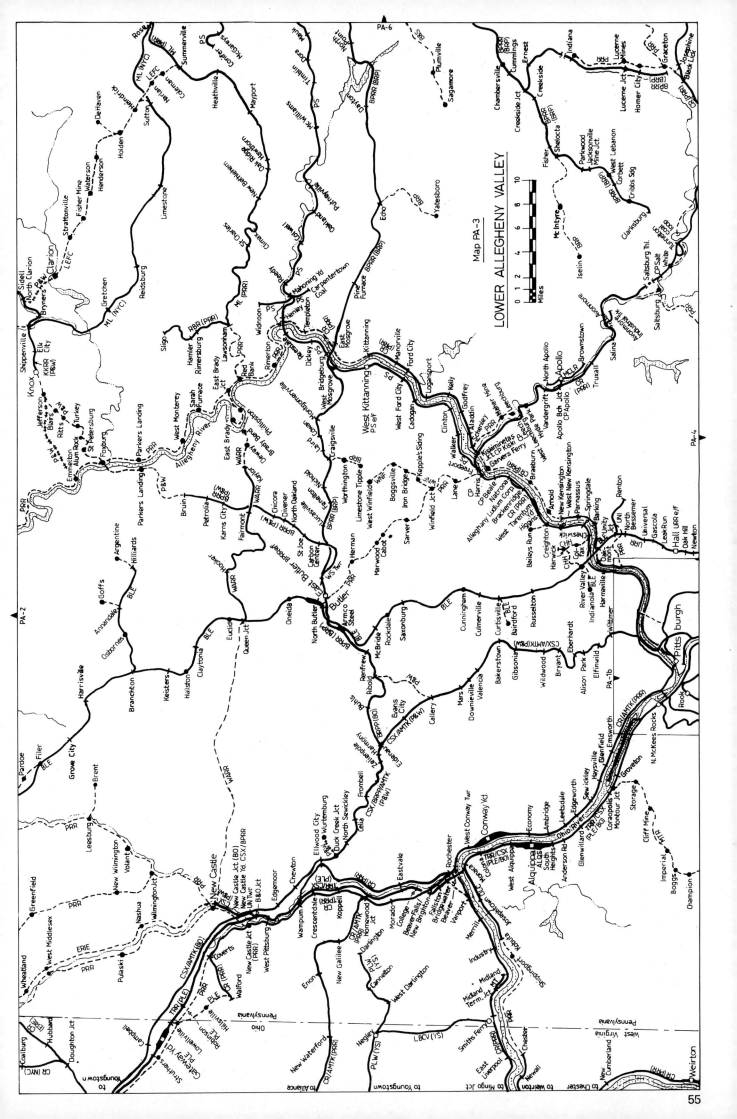

LOWER ALLEGHENY VALLEY

Map PA-3

Miles
0 1 2 4 6 8 10

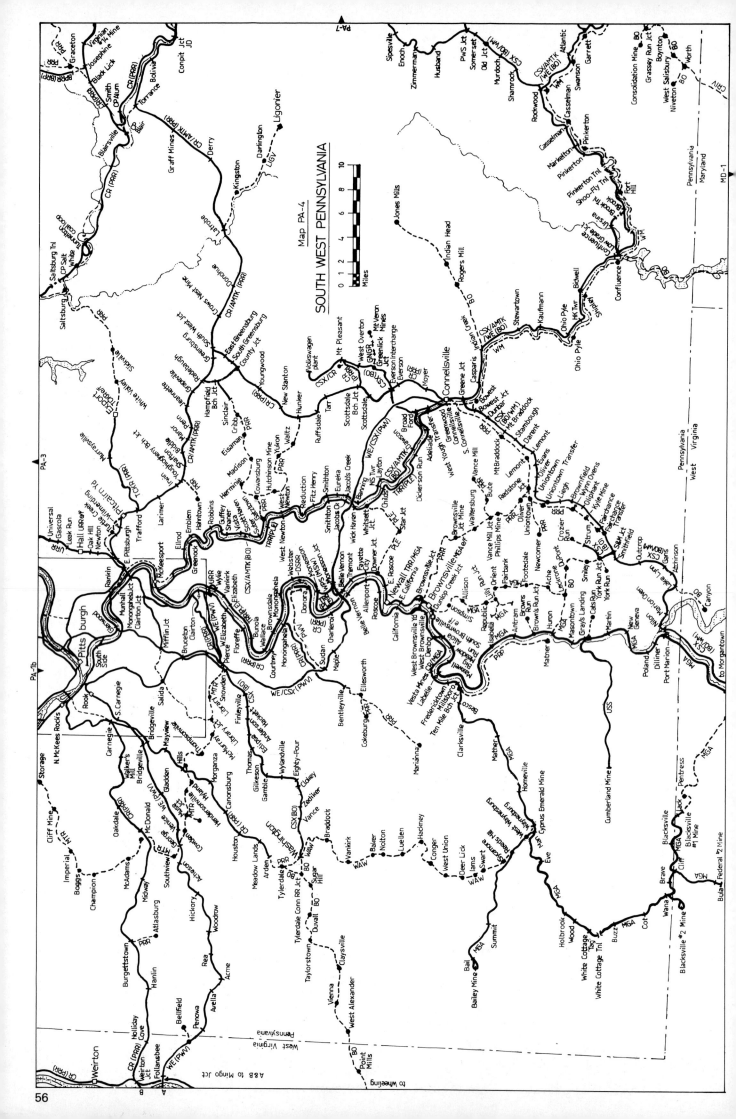

Map PA-4

SOUTH WEST PENNSYLVANIA

Miles
0 1 2   4   6   8   10

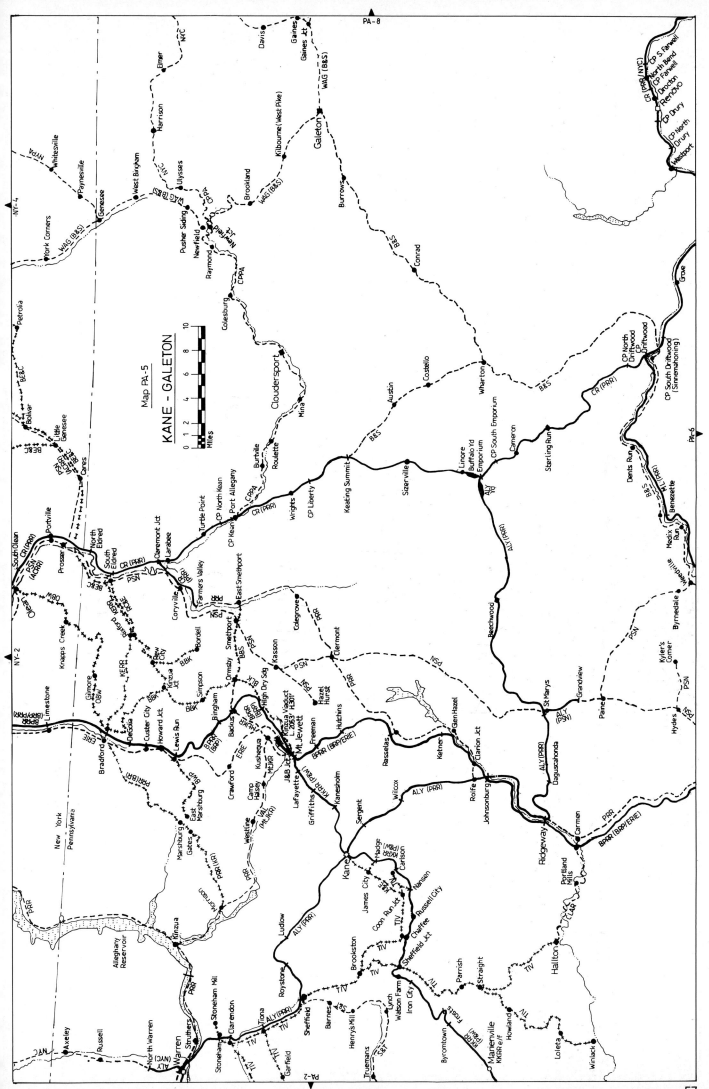

Map PA-5

KANE - GALETON

Miles

10 8 6 4 2 1 0

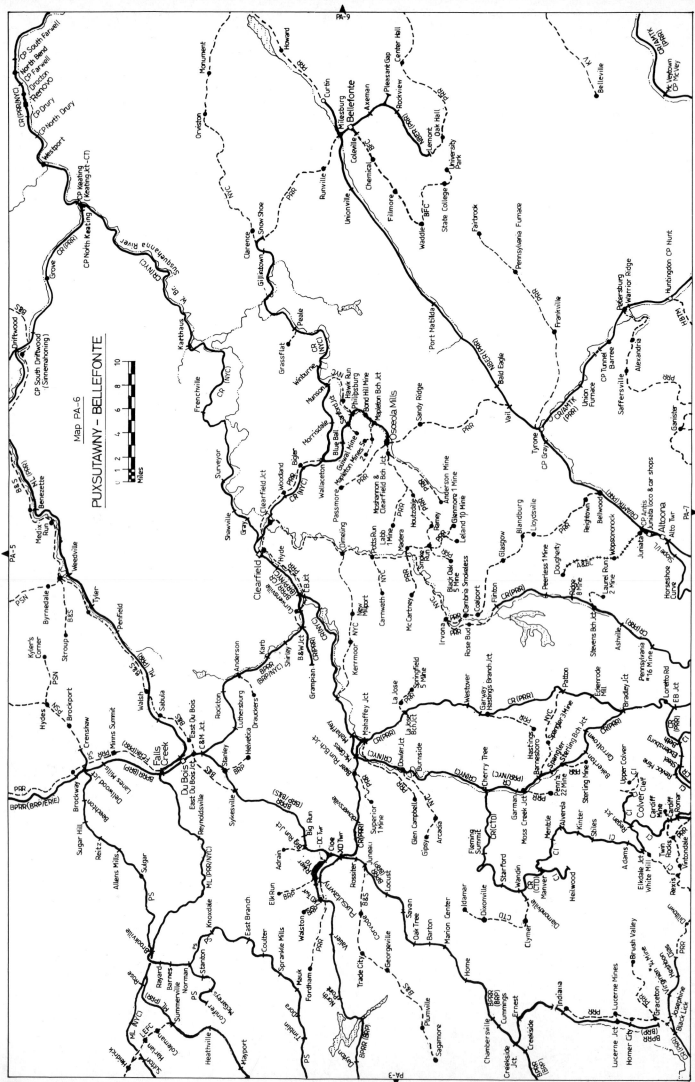

Map PA-6

PUXSUTAWNY – BELLEFONTE

0 1 2 4 6 8 10
Miles

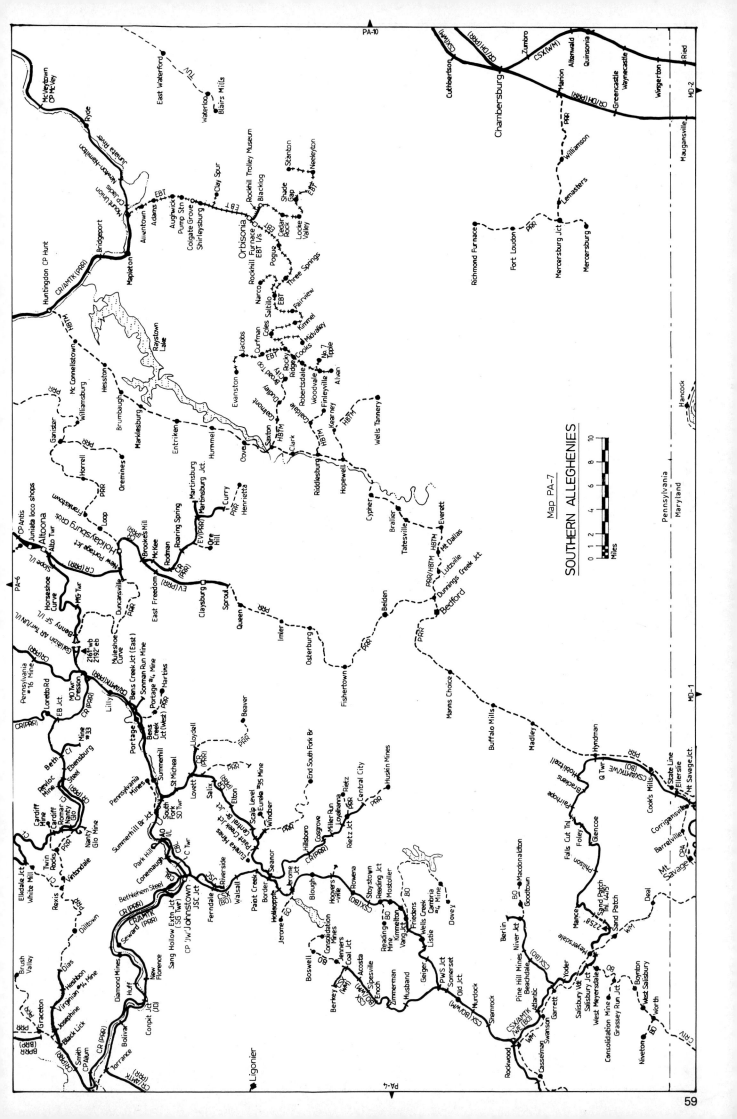

Map PA-7

SOUTHERN ALLEGHENIES

Pennsylvania
Maryland

59

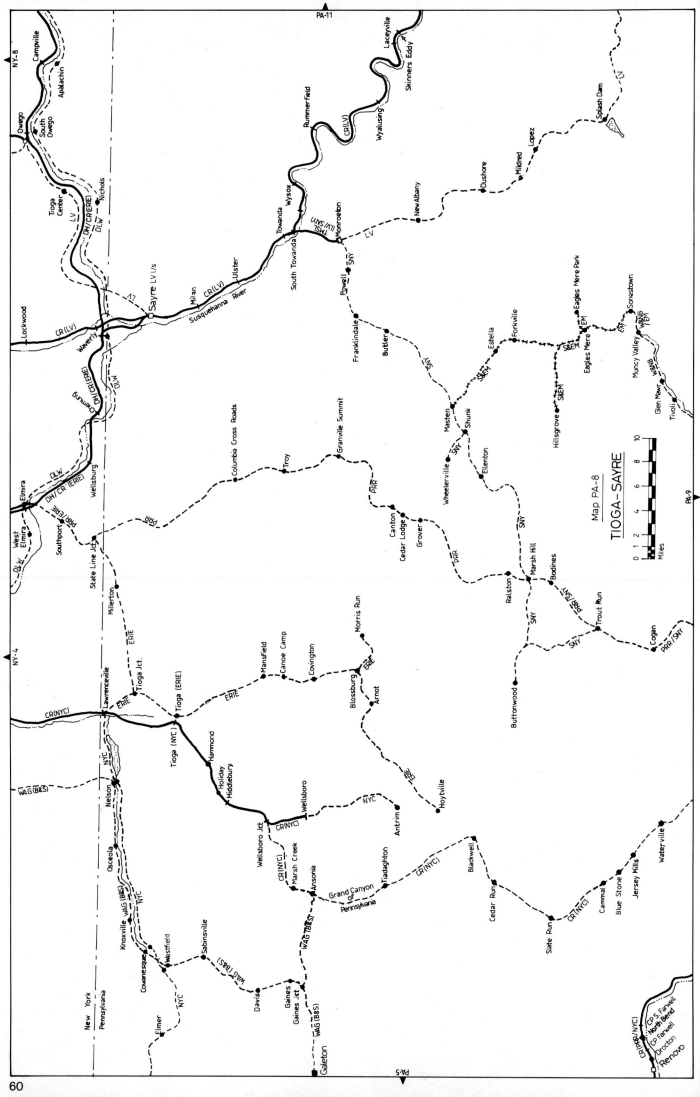

Map PA-8

TIOGA-SAYRE

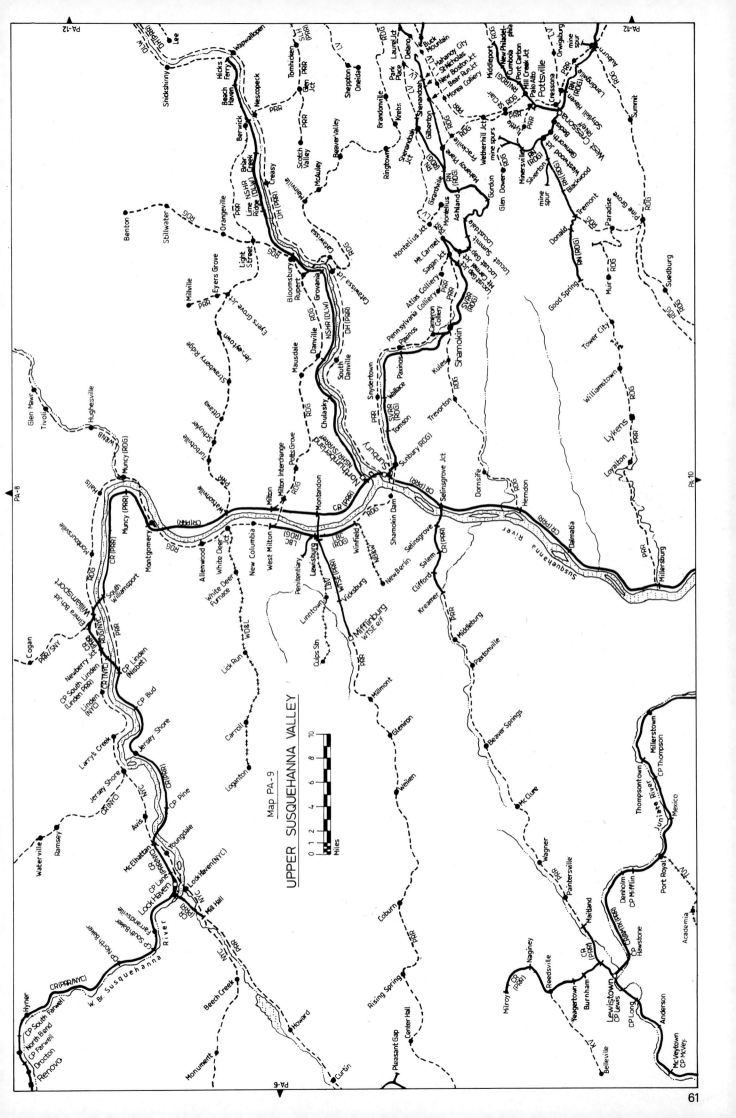

UPPER SUSQUEHANNA VALLEY

Map PA-9

Miles
0 1 2 4 6 8 10

61

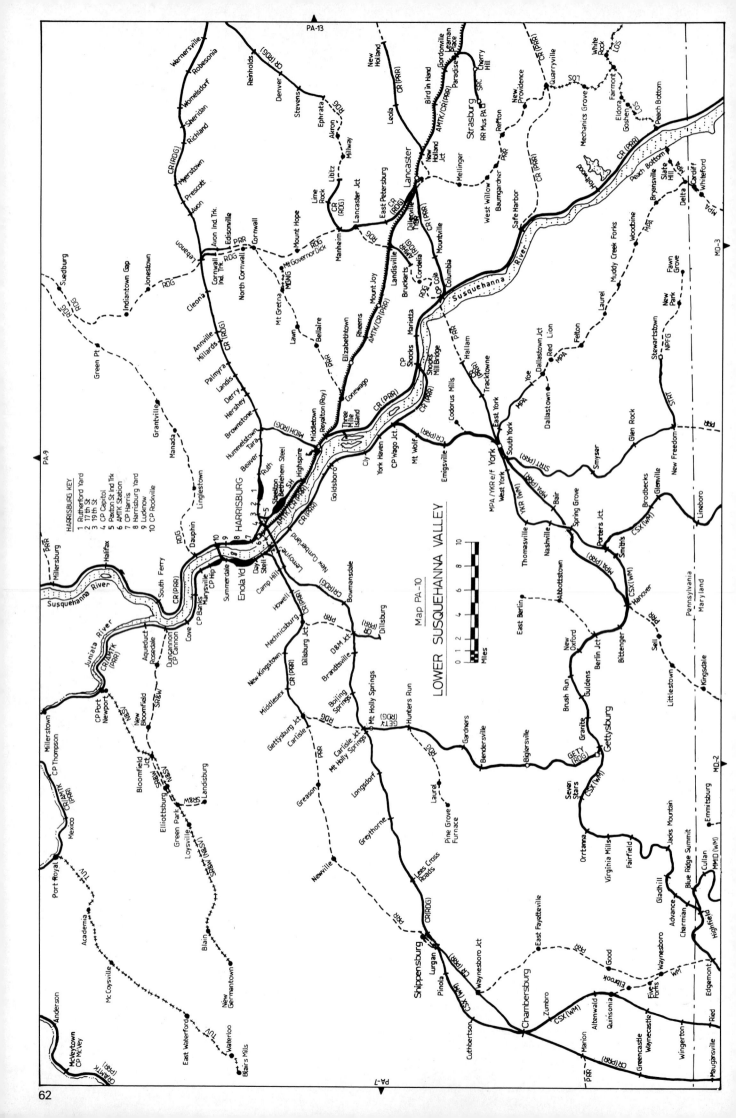

LOWER SUSQUEHANNA VALLEY

Map PA-10

Miles
0 1 2 4 6 8 10

HARRISBURG KEY
1 Rutherford Yard
2 17th St
3 19th St
4 CP Capitol
5 Paxton St Ind Trk
6 AMTK Station
7 CP Harris
8 Harrisburg Yard
9 Lucknow
10 CP Rodville

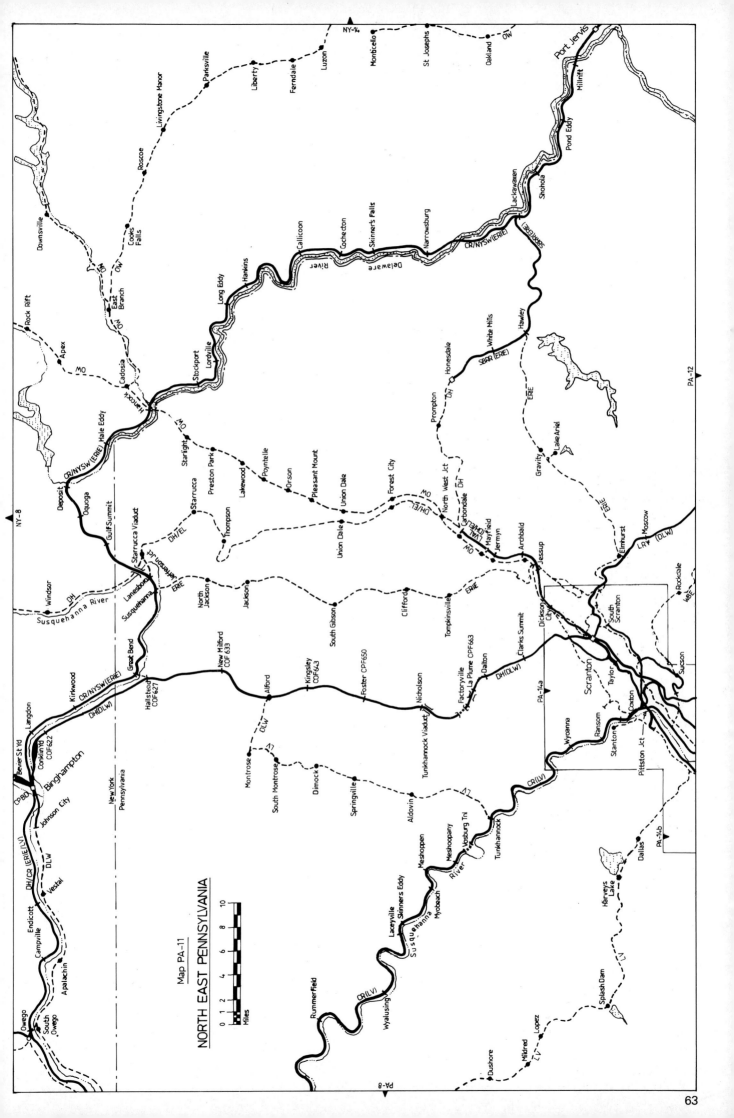

Map PA-11

NORTH EAST PENNSYLVANIA

Miles
0 1 2 3 4 6 8 10

63

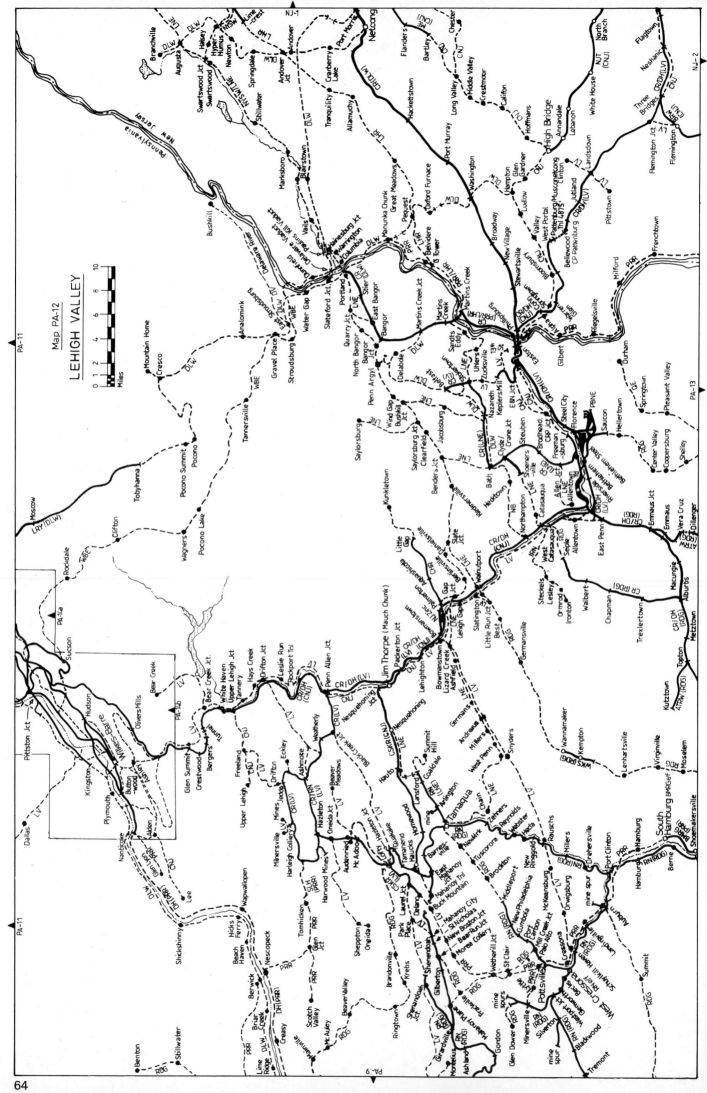

Map PA-12

LEHIGH VALLEY

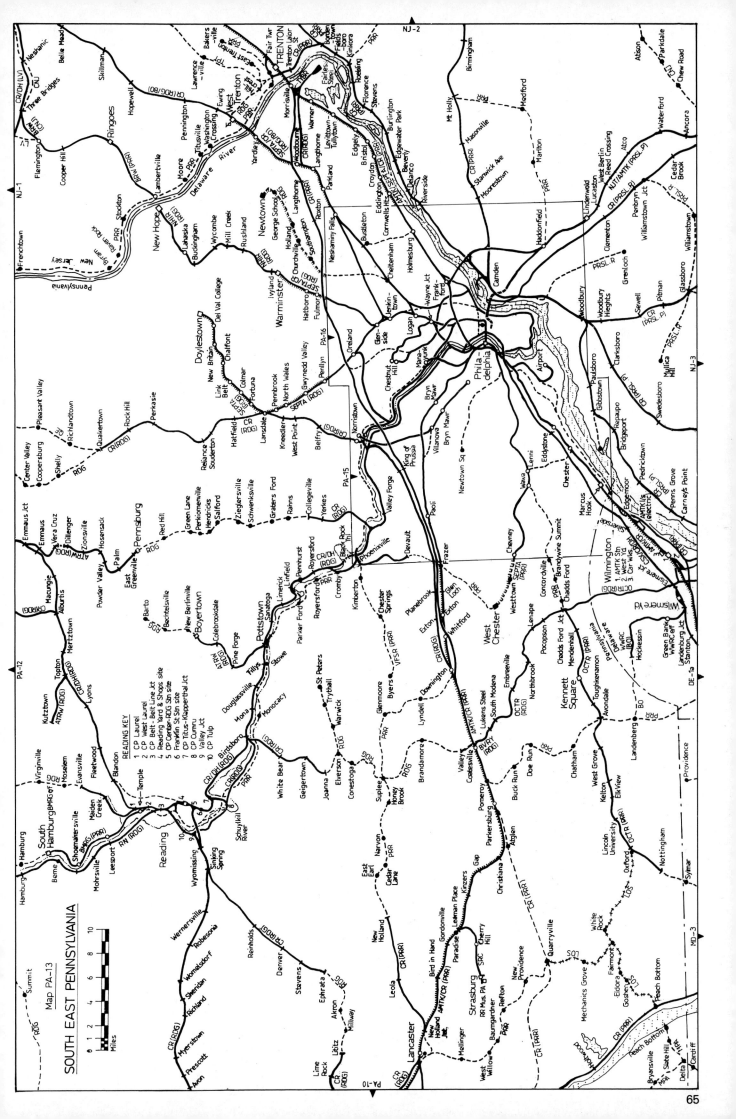

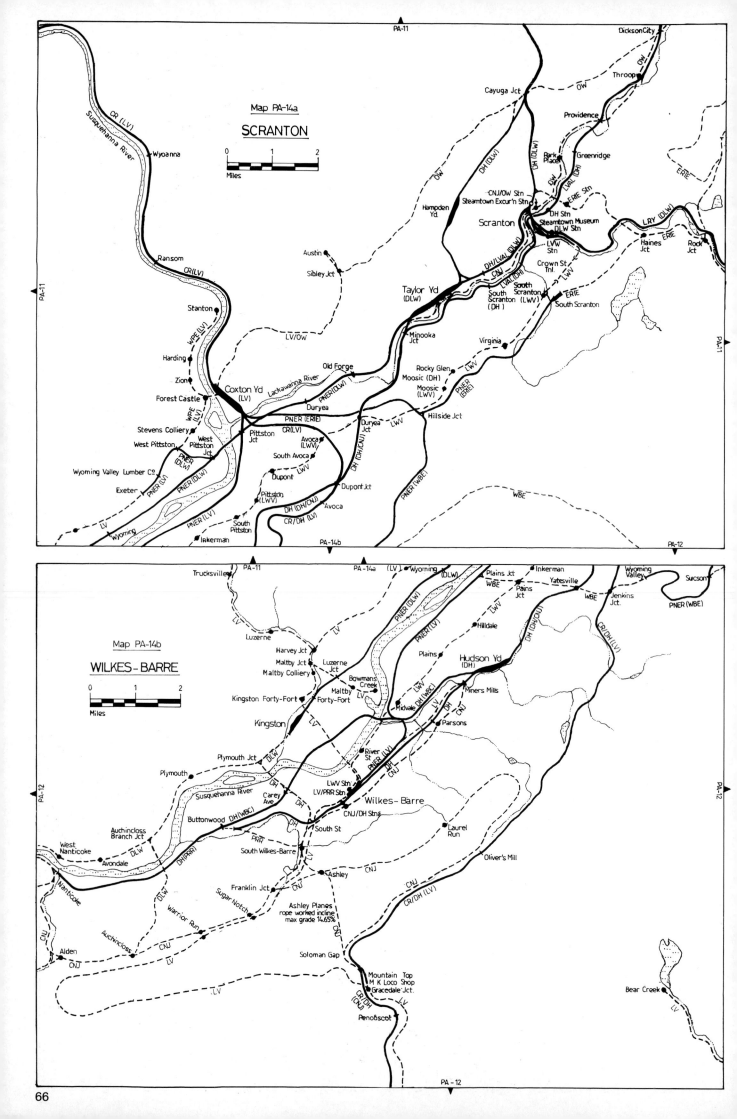

Map PA-14a

SCRANTON

0   1   2
Miles

Map PA-14b

WILKES-BARRE

0   1   2
Miles

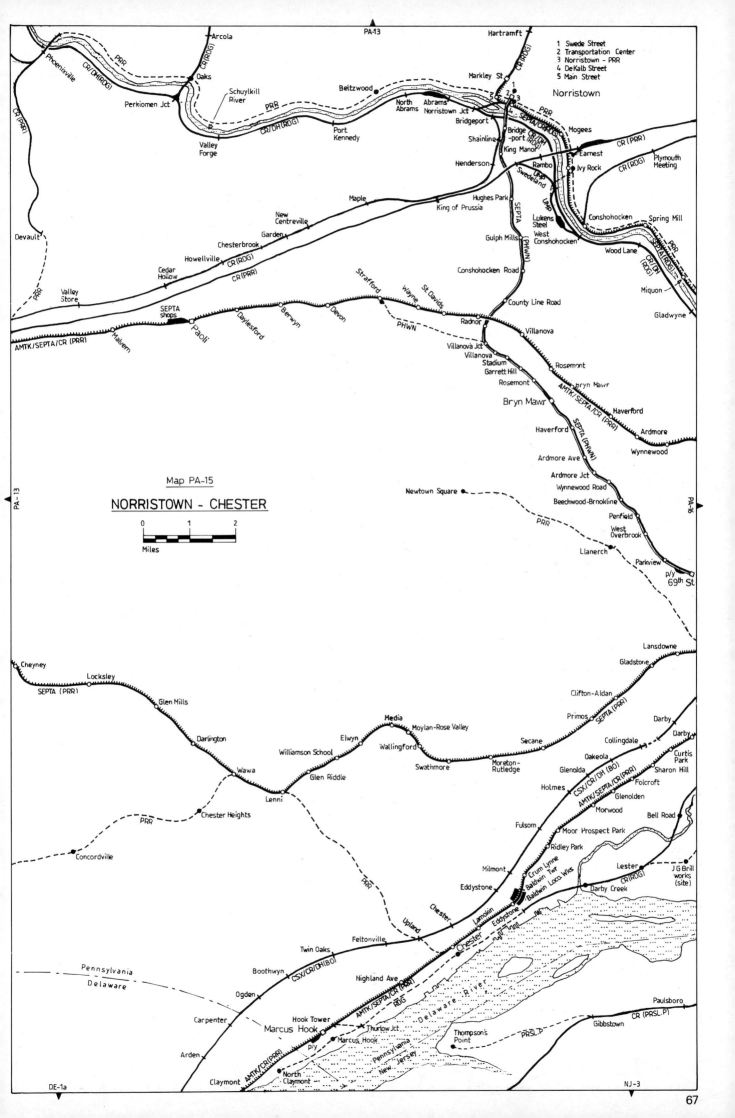

Map PA-15

NORRISTOWN - CHESTER

0   1   2
Miles

1 Swede Street
2 Transportation Center
3 Norristown - PRR
4 DeKalb Street
5 Main Street

Norristown

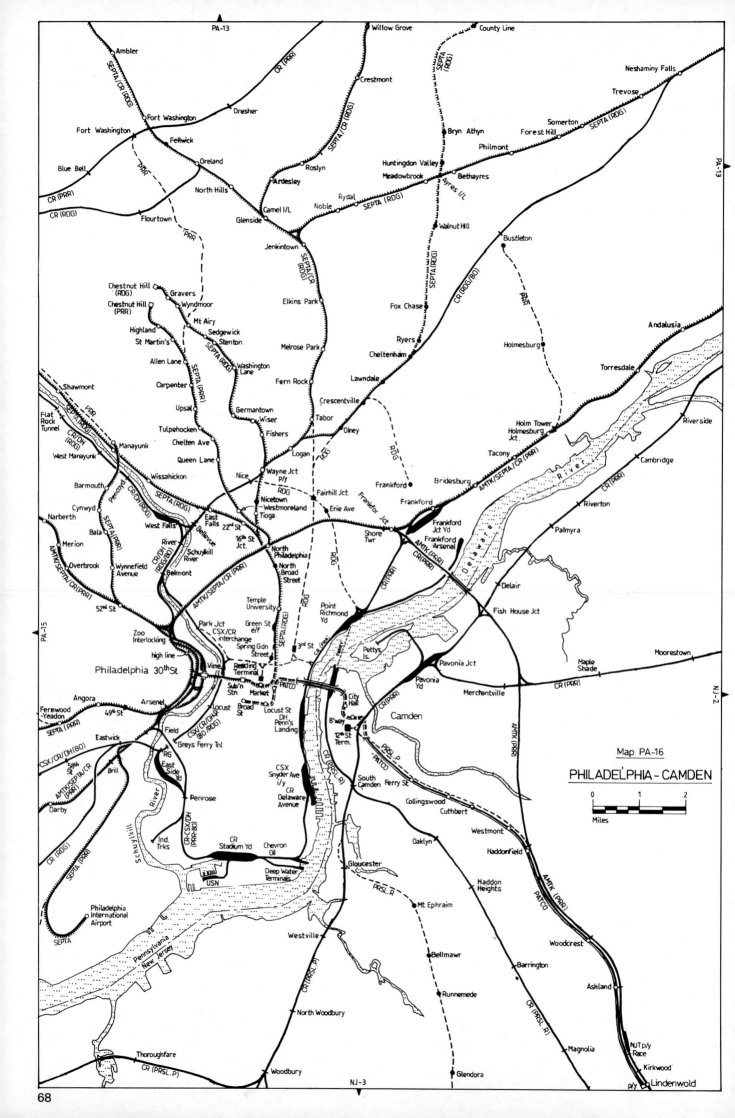

Map PA-16

PHILADELPHIA - CAMDEN

68

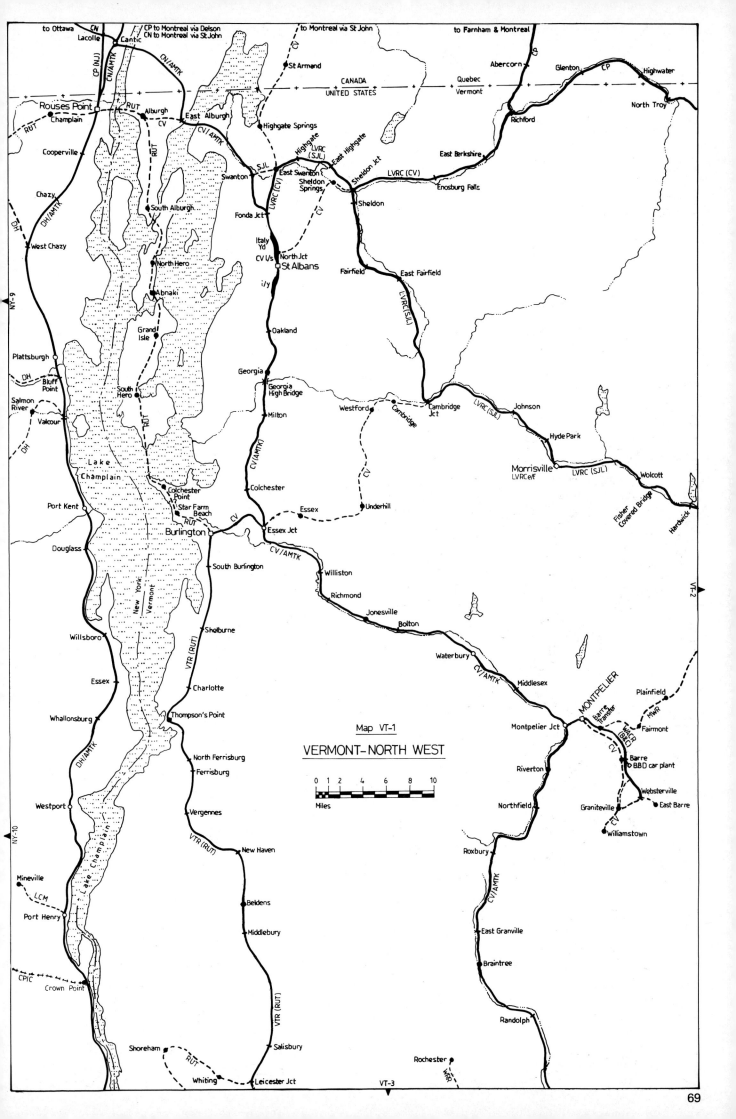

Map VT-1

VERMONT—NORTH WEST

0 1 2 4 6 8 10

Miles

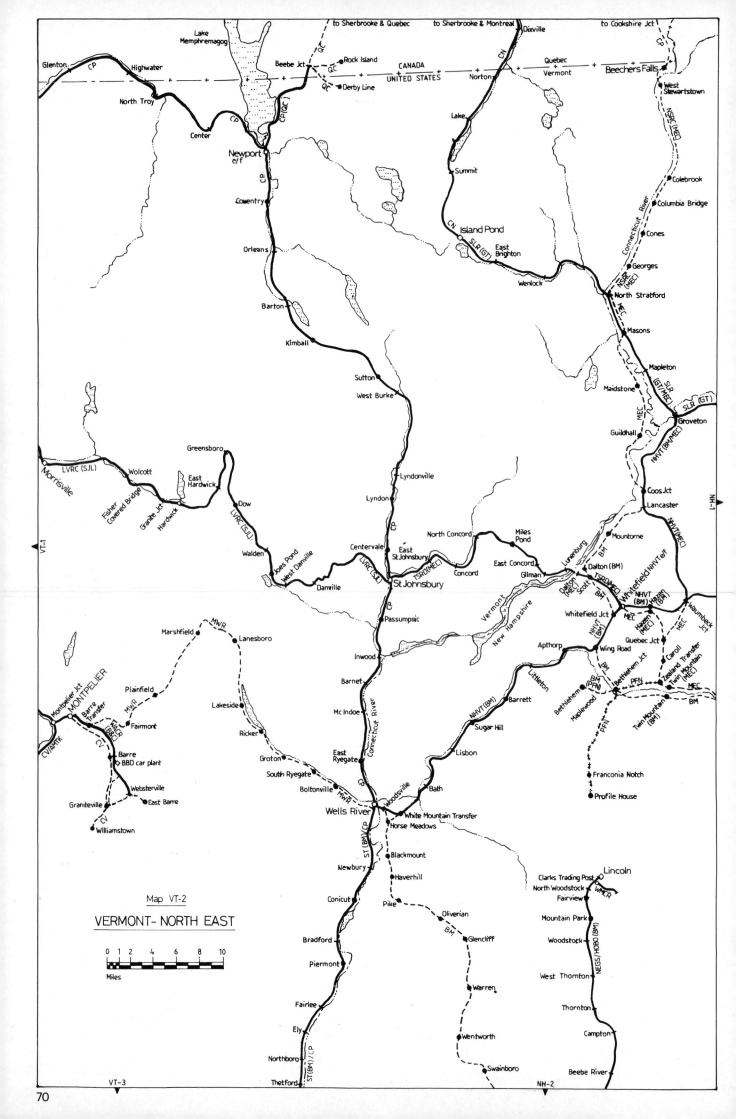

Map VT-2

VERMONT- NORTH EAST

Miles
0 1 2 4 6 8 10

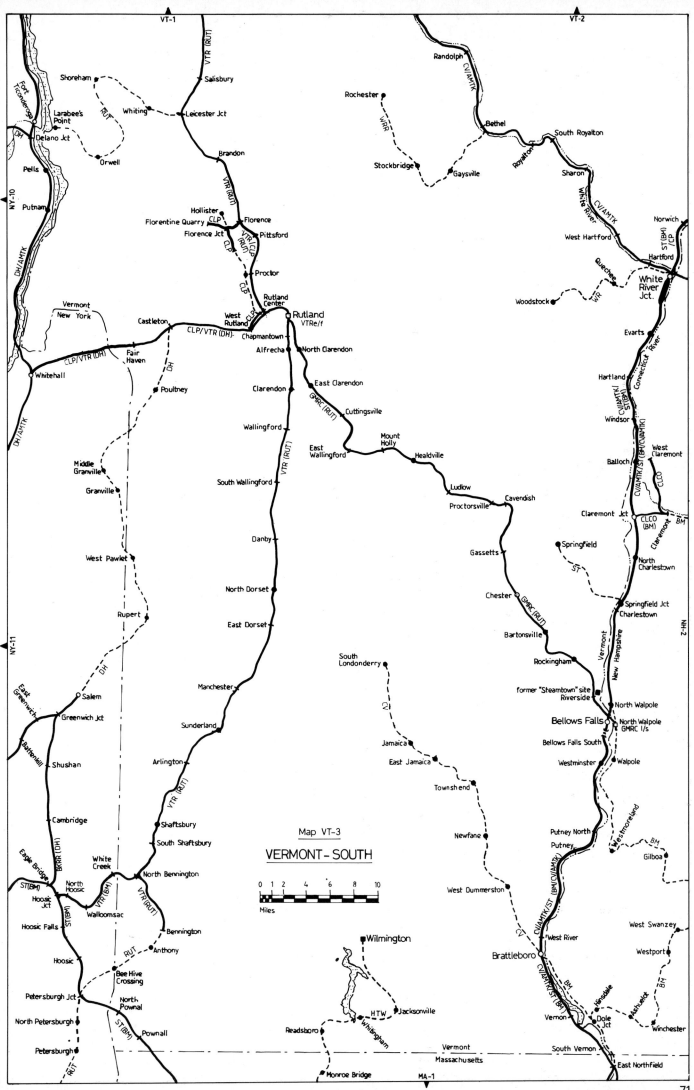

Map VT-3

VERMONT – SOUTH

0 1 2   4   6   8   10

Miles

71

Railroad Identification Marks

A & BC	Altoona & Beech Creek Railroad 3' gauge	CNYK	Central New York DO subsidery
ACRR	Allegany Central Railroad 3' gauge	CO	Chesapeake & Ohio Railway later CSX
ALBY	Albany Port Railroad CR-DH joint	CP	Canadian Pacific Railway
ALQS	Aliquippa & Southern Railroad	CPA	Cumberland & Pennsylvania Railroad later WM
ALY	Allegheny Railroad	CPIC	Crown Point Iron Co. 3' gauge
AMHR	Landisville Railroad - Amherst Industries	CPPA	Coudersport & Port Allegany Railroad
AMTK	Amtrak-National Railroad Passenger Corp.	CR	Conrail - Consolidated Railroad Corp.
ARA	Arcade & Attica Railroad	CRIV	Castleman River Railroad
ARDC	Adirondack Railway	CSKR	Carbon & Schylkill Railroad
ATRW	BMRG - previously Anthracite Railway	CSX	CSX Transportation
AVR	Aroostock Valley Railroad	CTD	Cherry Tree & Dixonville Railroad PRR - NYC joint
		CTN	Canton Railroad CV Central Vermont Railway
B & C	Barre & Chelsea Railroad		CN subsidary
B & H	Bridgton & Harrison Railway 2' gauge	CVAL	Central Valley Railroad 3' gauge
B & S	Buffalo & Susquehanna Railroad later BO	CWSR	Conway Scenic Railroad
B & SR	Bridgton & Saco River Railroad 2' gauge - later B & H		
BA	Boston & Albany NYC subsidary	DCLR	Delaware Coast Line Railroad
BAR	Bangor & Aroostock Railroad	DH	Delaware & Hudson Railway CP subsidary
BBK	Bradford Bordell & Kinzua Railroad 3'gauge	DLC	Duquesne Light Co. operated by PLE
BBS	Bradford Bordell & Smethport Railroad 3' gauge	DLW	Delaware Lackawanna & Western Railroad later E L
BCK	Buffalo Creek Railroad later CR	DLWR	Depew Lancaster & Western Railroad
BCLR	Bay Colony Railroad	DMM	Danville & Mount Morris Railroad GNWR subsidary
BE	Baltimore & Eastern PRR subsidary	DN	Delaware & Northern Railroad
BE & C	Bradford Eldred & Cuba Railroad 3' gauge	DO	Delaware Otsego Corp.
BEDT	Brooklyn East District Terminal	DSRR	Donora Southern Railroad
BFC	Bellefonte Central Railroad	DU	Delaware & Ulster Rail Ride
BH	Bath & Hammondsport Railroad	DV	Delaware Valley Railroad
BKRR	Batten Kill Railroad		
BLA	Baltimore & Annapolis Railroad	E & M	Etna & Montrose Railroad
BLE	Bessemer & Lake Erie Railroad	EBT	East Broad Top Railroad 3' gauge
BLK	Big Level & Kinzua Railroad 3' gauge	EEC	East Erie Commercial Railroad
BM	Boston & Maine Corp. GTI subsidary	EJR	East Jersey Railroad & Terminal
BML	Belfast & Moosehead Lake Railroad	EL	Erie-Lackawanna Railroad later CR
BMRG	Blue Mountain & Reading Railroad	EM	Eagles Mere Railroad 3' gauge
BMS	Berlin Mills Railway	EMIT	Emmitsburg Railroad
BO	Baltimore & Ohio Railroad later CSX	ERIE	Erie Railroad later EL
BPRR	Buffalo & Pittsburgh Railroad GNW subsidary	ESHR	Eastern Shore Railroad
BR	Bradford Railway 3' gauge	EV	Everett Railroad
BRBL	Boston Revere Beach & Lynn Railroad 2' gauge	EW	East Washington Railway
BRP	Buffalo Rochester & Pittsburgh Railway later BO		
BRVY	Brandywine Valley Raailroad	FCRK	Falls Creek RR
BRW	Black River & Western Corp.	FJG	Fonda Johnstone & Gloversville Railroad
BSR	Branford Steam Railway	FRY	Fore River Railway later QBT
BSOR	Buffalo Southern Railroad		
BT	Bush Terminal	GCC	Georges Creek & Cumberland Railroad
BWP	Bradford & Western Pennsylvania Railroad 3' gauge	GETY	Gettysburg Railroad
		GFOD	Great Falls & Old Dominion Railroad
C & T	Catskill & Tannersville Railroad 3' gauge	GJ	Greenwich & Johnsville Railway DH subsidary
CACV	Cooperstown & Charlotte Valley Railway	GMRC	Green Mountain Railroad
	DO subsidary	GNGR	Greenlick Narrow gauge Railroad 3' gauge
CAR	Canadian Atlantic Railway CP subsidary	GNWR	Genesee & Wyoming Railroad
CB	Chesapeake Beach Railroad	GR	Grasse River Railroad
CBL	Conemaugh & Black Lick Railroad	GT	Grand Trunk Railway CN subsidary
CCCL	Connecticut Central Railroad	GTI	Guilford Transportation Industries
CDOT	Connecticut Dept. of Transportation	GU	Grafton & Upton Railroad
CHH	Cheswick & Harmar Railroad		
CHR	Chestnut Ridge Railway	HBTM	Huntingdon & Broad Top Mountain Railroad
CI	Cambria & Indiana Railroad	HOBO	Hobo Railroad
CIARO	Ciaro RR 3' gauge	HRRC	Housatonic Railroad
CKM	Catskill Mountain Railroad	HSR	Hoboken Shore Road
CKMR	Catskill Mountain Railroad 3' gauge	HTW	Hoosac Tunnel & Wilmington Railroad
CLAR	Clarion River Railroad		
CLCO	Claremont Concord Railroad	IRN	Ironton Railroad later CR
CLP	Claremont & Pittsford Railroad		
CN	Canadian National Railways	JCLE	Jamestown Chautauqua & Lake Erie Railroad
CNJ	Central RR of New Jersey later CR	JSC	Johnstown & Stoney Creek Railroad operated by CR
		JSCR	Jay Street Connecting Railroad

K & E	Kane & Elk Railroad 3' gauge
KC	Kennebec Central Railroad 2' gauge
KKRR	Knox & Kane RR
KNOX	Knox Railroad
KR	Kinzua Railway 3' gauge
KRR	Kaaterskill Railroad 3' gauge
KV	Kishacoquillas Valley Railroad
LAL	Livonia Avon & Lakeville Railroad
LASB	Lackawaxen & Stourbridge Railroad DO subsidary, later SBRR
LBC	Lewisburg & Buffalo Creek Railroad
LBCV	Little Beaver Creek Valley Railroad PLW subsidary
LBR	Lowville & Beaver River Railroad
LBV	Lewisburg & Buffalo Valley Railroad 3' gauge
LCM	Lake Champlain & Moriah Railroad
LEFC	Lake Erie Franklin & Clarion Railroad
LHR	Lehigh & Hudson River Railway later CR
LIGV	Ligonier Valler Railroad
LIRR	Long Island Railroad MTA subsidary
LNE	Lehigh & New England Railroad
LOS	Lancaster Oxford & Southern Railroad 3' gauge
LRY	Lackawanna Railway LVAL subsidary
LSMS	Lake Shore & Michigan Southern NYC subsidary
LV	Lehigh Valley Railroad later CR
LVAL	Lackawanna Valley Railroad
LWV	Lackawanna & Wyoming Valley Railroad
M & S	Middleburg & Schoharie Railroad
MARC	Maryland Dept. of Transportation
MBRR	Milton - Bennington Railroad
MBTA	Massachusetts Bay Transportation Authority
MC	Michigan Central NYC subsidary
MCER	Massachusetts Central Railroad
MCLR	McLaughlin Line Railroad
MCRR	Monongahela Connecting Railroad
MCST	Maine Coast Railroad
MDDE	Maryland & Delaware Railroad
ME	Morristown & Erie Railway
MEC	Maine Central Railroad GTI subsidary
MGA	Monongahela Railway CR subsidary
MGNG	Mt Gretna Narrow Gauge Railway 2' gauge
MHM	Mount Hope Mineral Railroad CNJ subsidary
MHWA	Mohawk Adirondack & Northern Railroad
MIDH	Middletown & Hummelstown Railroad
MKC	McKeesport Connecting Railroad
ML	Mountain Laurel Railroad PS subsidary
MMID	Maryland Midland Railway
MNC	Metro North Commuter MTA subsidary
MNJ	Middletown & New Jersey Railway
MOL	Marcellus & Otisco Lakes Railroad
MONS	Monson Railroad 2' gauge
MOV	Moshassuck Valley Railroad
MPA	Maryland & Pennsylvania Railroad
MSTR	Massena Terminal Railroad
MSW	Monesson South Western Railroad
MtJKR	Mt Jewett Kinzua & Riterville Railroad 3' gauge
MtWR	Mt Washington Railway Rack & Pinion Std gauge
MT	Midland Terminal
MTA	Metropolitain Transportation Authority
MTR	Montour Railroad
MVYD	Martha's Vineyard Railroad 3' gauge
MWR	Montpelier & Wells River Railroad
N & SV	Newport & Sherman's Valley Railroad 3' gauge
NAN	Nantucket Railroad 3' gauge
NAP	Narragansett Pier Railroad
NB	Northampton & Bath Railroad

NB & W	New Berlin & Winfield Railroad 3' gauge
NBER	Nittany & Bald Eagle Railroad
NCS	Newark City Subway later NJT
NEGS	New England Southern Railroad
NH	New York New Haven & Hartford Railroad later PC
NHIR	New Hope & Ivyland Railroad
NHNC	New Hampshire North Coast Corp.
NHT	New Haven Terminal
NHVT	New Hampshire & Vermont Railroad
NIAJ	Niagara Junction Railway later CR
NJ	Napierville Junction Railway DH subsidary
NJNY	New Jersey & New York Railroad Erie subsidary
NJT	New Jersey Transit
NKP	Nickel Plate - New York Chicago & St Louis later NW
NLI	National Lead Industries
NPFG	New Park & Fawn Grove Railroad
NS	Norfolk Southern Corp.
NSHR	North Shore RR
NSL	Norwood & St Lawrence Railroad
NSRC	North Streatford Railroad
NW	Norfolk & Western later NS
NYC	New York Central later PC
NYCH	New York Cross Harbor Railroad Terminal
NYCR	New York Connecting Railroad LIRR-NH-PRR joint
NYCTA	New York City Transit Authority MTA subsidary
NYD	New York Dock Co.
NYGL	New York & Greenwood Lake Railway Erie subsidary
NYLB	New York & Long Branch Railroad CNJ-PRR joint
NYLE	New York & Lake Erie Railroad
NYSW	New York Susquehanna & Western Railway DO subsidary
OB&W	Olean Bradford & Warren Railway 3' gauge
OCTL	Oil City & Titusville Lines
OCTR	Octoraro Railway
OER	Otis Elevating Railway funicular 3' gauge
OMID	Ontario Midland Railroad
ONCR	Ontario Central Railroad
ONER	Ontario Easton Railroad
OW	New York Ontario & Western Railroad
P & W	Pittsburgh & Western Railroad 3' gauge
PAM	Pittsburgh Allegheny & McKees Rock Railroad
PATCO	Port Authority Transit Corp.
PATH	Port Authority Trans-Hudson
PAUT	Philadelphia & Atlantic Railroad PRR subsidary
PBNE	Philadelphia Bethlehem & New England Railroad
PBR	Patapsco & Back Rivers Railroad
PC	Penn Central Transportation Co. later CR
PCY	Pittsburgh Chartiers & Youghiogheny Railway
PFN	Profile & Franconia Notch Railroad 3' gauge
PHWN	Philadelphia & Western SEPTA subsidary
PJR	Port Jersey Railroad
PLE	Pittsburgh & Lake Erie Railroad NYC subsidary, later TRR
PLW	Pittsburgh Lisbon & Western Railroad
PM	Pere Marquette Railway later CO
PNER	Pocono Northeast Railway
POTED	Potomac Edison Co.
POV	Pittsburgh & Ohio Valley Railway
PRES	Preston Railroad
PRR	Pennsylvania Railroad later PC
PRSL.P	Pennsylvania-Reading Seashore Lines ex- PRR later CR
PRSL.R	Pennsylvania-Reading Seashore Lines ex-RDG later CR
PS	Pittsburg & Shawmut Railroad
PSN	Pittsburg Shawmut & Northern Railroad
PVAL	Panther Valley Railroad later CSKR

PVRR	Pioneer Valley Railroad	TSRD	Twin States Railroad LVRC subsidary
PW	Providence & Worcester Railroad	TUV	Tuscarora Valley & Cuba Railroad 3' gauge
PWJ	West Jersey Railroad	TVC	Tonawanda Valley & Cuba Railroad 3' gauge
PWV	Pittsburgh & West Virginia Railway later NW	TYBR	Tyburn Railroad
QBT	Quincy Bay Terminal NEGS subsidary	UD	Ulster & Delaware Railroad later NYC
QC	Quebec Central Railway CP subsidary	UFRR	Union Freight Railroad BM-NH-NYC joint
QE	Quakertown & Eastern Railroad	UMP	Upper Merion & Plymouth Railroad
		UNI	Unity Railways BLE operated
R	Rockport Railroad 3' gauge	URR	Union Railroad
RBR	Red Bank Railroad PS subsidary	USA	United States Army
RCE	Rew City & Eldred Railroad 3' gauge	USAF	United States Air Force
RDG	Reading Company later CR	USCG	United States Coast Guard
RFP	Richmond Fredericksburg & Potomac Railway CSX subsidary	USG	United States Gov't. Dept of Defence
		USN	United States Navy
RN	Reading Blue Mountain & Northern Railroad	USS	United States Steel Corp.
RR	Raritan River Railroad later CR	UV	Unadilla Valley Railway
RSR	Rochester & Southern Railroad GNWR subsidary		
RUT	Rutland Railroad	VAC	Virginia Central Railway
RV	Rahway Valley Railroad DO subsidary	VAL	Valley Railroad
		VALE	Connecticut Valley Railroad
S & EM	Susquehanna & Eagles Mere Railroad 3' gauge	VFSR	Valley Falls Scenic Railroad
S & S	Saratoga & Schuylerville Railroad BM subsidary	VIA	VIA Rail Canada
S & T	Sheffield & Tionesta Railroad	VRE	Virginia Railway Express - Virginia Dept. of Transport
SB	South Buffalo Railway		
SBK	South Brooklyn Railway MTA subsidary	VTR	Vermont Railway
SBRR	Stourbridge Railroad		
SBVR	South Branch Valley Railroad	W & NB	Williamsport & North Branch Railroad
SCCM	Stony Clove & Catskill Mountain Railroad 3' gauge	WAB	Wabash Railroad later NW
SEPTA	South-eastern Pennsylvania Transportation Authority	WACR	Washington County Railroad
		WAG	Wellsville Addison & Galeton Railroad
SERR	Sanford & Eastern Railroad BM subsidary	WARR	Western Alleghany Railroad later BLE
SFLR	Shore Fast Line Inc.	WAW	Waynesburg & Washington Railroad 3' gauge
SH	Steelton & Highspire Railroad	WBC	Wilkes- Bare Connecting Railroad DH subsidary
SIRT	Staten Island Rapid Transit MTA Subsidary	WBC	Wilkes-Bare & Eastern Railroad NYSW subsidary
SIRY	Staten Island Railway DO subsidary	WD & L	White Deer & Loganton 3' gauge
SJL	St Johnsbury & Lamoile County Railroad	WE	Wheeling & Lake Erie Railway 1990 regional
SLAW	St Lawrence Railroad	WHN	Wharton & Northern Railroad CNJ subsidary
SLH	Sugar Loaf & Hazleton Railroad	WJSL	West Jersey Short Line later PWJ
SLR	St Lawrence & Atlantic Railroad	WKS	Wanamaker Kempton & Southern Railroad
SLRR	St Lawrence & Raquette River Railroad	WLE	Wheeling & Lake Erie Railway later NW
SMMLG	Saratoga Mt McGregar & Lake George Railroad	WLFB	Wolfeboro Railroad
SNY	Susquehanna & New York Railroad	WM	Western Maryland Railway later CSX
SOM	Somerset Railroad CR operated	WMCR	White Mountain Central Railroad
SONY	Southern New York Railway	WMS	Western Maryland Scenic Railroad
SOU	Southern Railway later NS	WNF	Winifrede Railroad
SR & W	Susquehanna River & Western Railroad	WOD	Washington & Old Dominion Railroad
SRC	Strasburg Railroad	WPE	West Pittston - Exeter Railroad
SRRL	Sandy River & Rangeley Lakes Railroad 2' gauge	WPS	Wheeling Pittsburgh Steel
SSL	Skaneatles Short Line Railroad	WR	Woodstock Railroad
SSRR	Springrille & Sardinia Railroad 3' gauge	WRB	Wood River Branch Railroad
ST	Springfield Terminal GTI subsidary	WRR	White River Railroad
STN	Steamtown Museum	WRWK	Warwick Railway
STRT	Stewartstown Railroad	WS	West Shore Route NYC subsidary
SV	Suncook Valley Railroad BM subsidary	WT	Washington Terminal Co. BO-CO-SOU-PRR joint later AMTK
SVRR	Shamokin Valley Railroad		
TCRK	Turtle Creek Industrial Railroad	WTSE	West Shore Railroad
THB	Toronto Hamilton & Buffalo Railway later CP	WW	Winchester & Western Railroad- Virginia Division
TIOC	Tioga Central Railroad	WWF	Wiscasset Waterville & Farmington Railroad 2' gauge
TIRL	Tonawanda Island Railroad		
TIV	Tionesta Valley Railroad 3' gauge	WWN	Wincester & Western Railroad - New Jersey Division
TM&P	Twin Mountain & Potomac 3' gauge	WWRC	Wilmington & Western Railroad
TMC	Temiscouata Railway later CN		
TMSL	Tonawanda-Monpoeton Shippers Lifeline	YKR	Yorkrail Inc.
TNY	Trolley Museum of New York	YS	Youngstown & Southern Railway later PLW
TPT	Trenton-Princeton Traction Co RDG subsidary		
TRR	Three Rivers Railway CSX subsidary		

NOTES

NOTES